William J. Short OFM

The Franciscans

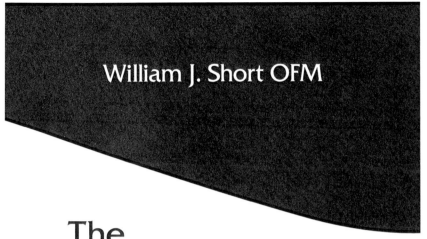

TAU

The Franciscans
William J. Short, OFM

Cover images: Shutetrstock.com, Illustration by Vincent Ngueyn, Photo of St. Francis Statue by Brian Buettner
Cover and book design: Tau Publishing Design Department

For information regarding permission, write to:
Tau Publishing, LLC
Attention: Permissions Dept.
4727 North 12th street
Phoenix, AZ 85014

ISBN 978-1-61956-121-2

First Edition April 2013
10 9 8 7 6 5 4 3 2 1

Published and printed in the United States of America by Tau Publishing, LLC
For additional inspirational books visit us at Tau-Publishing.com

TauPublishing.com
Words of Inspiration

To the memory of my parents,
Marjorie Ellen and William Thomas Short,
who first taught me what it means to be
a Franciscan

Contents

Foreword   iii

Introduction   vii

1 The Founders: Francis and Clare   1

2 The Lesser Brothers and Their Various Branches   29

3 The Poor Sisters: Growth and Reform   79

4 Brothers and Sisters of Penance   97

5 The Franciscan Spirit   119

6 Franciscans Today   155

Subject Index   173

Foreword

When I was first invited to write this book, I readily accepted. After several years of work, I now realize how little I knew then and how much I have yet to learn. I had thought that the task would be fairly modest: to introduce the Franciscans to readers who might wonder who we are. The task became more complex as I tried to determine those to whom the word "Franciscan" was applied. At first, I suppose, I meant to write about the men belonging to the Order of Friars Minor (OFM), the Order of Friars Minor Capuchin (OFMCap), and the Order of Friars Minor Conventual (OFMConv).

I realized, however, that our story would be incomplete, and the name "Franciscan" too narrowly applied if I wrote only of the men of the "First Order." Franciscan religious women far outnumber the men, and they have received scant attention in some treatments of Franciscan life and mission. To write about the followers of St. Clare was an unexpected pleasure, exposing me, however superficially, to a story of courage and constantly renewed ideals.

There are many other communities of Franciscan women

religious besides the Poor Clares. The task of sketching the life and work of Franciscan sisters was difficult, and sources were often unavailable. I have outlined in this work what I hope may become a history of Franciscan women's congregations of the Third Order Regular.

Yet another dimension of my task appeared in my meeting with Fr. Raffaele Pazzelli, TOR, and my study of his works on the Brothers and Sisters of Penance, the Third Order, in its lay and religious forms, the Secular Franciscan Order and the Third Order Regular. Work here is still incomplete, and the English-speaking world in particular must promote further studies of these important members of the Penitents' movement.

What have I learned from these three years of study, alternated with teaching and travel? I hope that I have learned some humility. I can take little credit for the contents of this book. My work has been that of a compiler, at times that of a translator. Others have done the hard work of primary research: I have assembled what they have learned and published. I am only too aware that much has been omitted because of the introductory character of this work. It is a book for beginners, not for proficients.

Besides humility, I have learned gratitude. The friars of the Capuchin Historical Institute generously hosted me at their home outside Rome. Fr. Wayne Hellmann, OFMConv, and the Conventual friars in St. Louis offered books, advice and encouragement. Fr. Cesare Vaiani, OFM, of the *Biblioteca Francescana* in Milan gave me free copies of everything I needed (and wonderful meals). Fr. Regis Armstrong, OFMCap, and Sr. Margaret Carney, OSF, shared with me their continuing research on St. Clare. My confreres at the *Collegio Sant' Antonio* and the OFM General Curia in Rome gave me keys to their libraries. Fr. Giorgio Vigna, OFM, and the

Province of St. Bonaventure in Piedmont gave me a sabbatical marked by good wine, good humor and books without limit. The Franciscan Sisters of Philadelphia, Pennsylvania; Clinton, Iowa; and Redwood City, California, endured my faltering steps toward clarity. My Belgian Franciscan brother, Jean-François Godet, gave me good example and good advice on the Franciscan life.

My colleagues and students at the Franciscan School of Theology graciously embraced a sometimes distracted dean, then president, with a *cortesia* that would have charmed St. Francis.

Kristeen Bruun remained convinced, at times when I was not, that the project could be completed. Her hard work put the manuscript into intelligible form, enriched by good advice.

Michael Downey read the drafts, corrected, advised, encouraged and assured, claiming even to have learned from the travail. Joseph Chinnici modelled patient scholarly responsibility, endured my fretting and applauded my progress.

With humble thanks, I offer to my Franciscan brothers and sisters the fruit of these years of reading, reflection and conversation. During this time I have been privileged to learn more about my own religious family, many of whose members I know because of this book. I hope that these pages may now allow others to know this family, and to love it as I do.

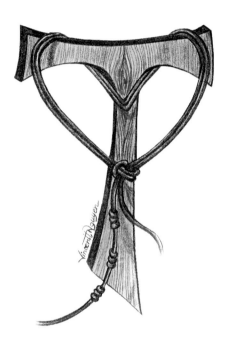

Introduction

The Franciscans: Who are they? How did they start? How have they grown? What do they do? What do they believe? Where are they today?

These are some of the questions this book will try to answer. And in answering those questions it will sketch a family portrait, that of the Franciscans, a picture of a family with its own memories, its own character, its own stories. Some of these stories are familiar to many; other stories, even some of the best, remain unknown. And one good reason for writing a book like this one is to tell those stories to a new audience who may find in them a reason to give thanks, or be surprised, or even smile.

But our time is only that of a long evening's reading, perhaps two—which stories to tell? Start at the beginning or in the middle? Only happy endings? Who will be included? The answers to these questions will come only at the end of the last story. And by that time, if the audience is pleased, they will forgive much that was imperfect in the telling.

It may be best to start with a nut tree, a family, and a basilica.

Many years ago, in a wooden tree-house he built in a walnut

tree, a Scripture professor was reading the Gospel of John. He had chosen the walnut tree because, scholar that he was, this Portuguese priest knew it kept the summer's mosquitoes away. He was preparing a series of homilies to be preached that Lent in Northern Italy, in the area near Venice.

Seven hundred years later, within thin walls of wood and corrugated tin, a picture of that preacher hangs in the home of a tenant farmer's family in the Northeast of Brazil. They belong to the same family as the Scripture professor.

The computer screens in the editorial offices show the last corrections in the magazine's layout. The offices are near the basilica, dedicated to the same preacher, buried there, in Padua. The office workers belong to that family too.

And the preacher from Portugal now known as St. Anthony belongs to their family because he, like the family in Brazil and the office workers in Italy, could look back to a common heritage they share: they are all Franciscans.

On a single day of this year, in places far from each other, a set of snapshots could show us other parts of this family.

A barefoot woman enters a sparsely furnished chapel. Her life is contemplative, and is marked by silence and work. She and her sisters live in Malawi, and they belong to that family called the Franciscans.

A man and a woman driving to work on a California highway: they work on a farm as seasonal harvesters. They have been married for ten years and have two small children. They belong to the same family as the sisters in Malawi.

Four men revising a document in Rome: one is from Spain, one from the United States, and two from Italy. They are generals of four religious orders. And they belong to the same family.

In Manila, thirty delegates of different women's religious congregations meet at a break during a conference. All of them belong to the same family.

In any family album, the snapshots multiply as if they had a life of their own, one generating another. Here too, the pictures could be many more. With these glimpses of a day in the life of the Franciscan Family, the diversity of its members is apparent. These are men and women, lay and religious, contemplative and active, belonging to communities, each with its own history. Yet they hold in common a heritage, a common symbolic language, and are related to each other through intricate lines of kinship. All belong to a family whose beginnings they can trace to Francis of Assisi, to Clare of Assisi, and to a group of penitents of Assisi: the members of a renewal movement in a small town of central Italy in the thirteenth century.

The Franciscan population has grown enormously since then. From a handful of brothers and sisters in the early 1200s, the number has grown to some 1.5 million today, in a myriad of organizations, orders, communities and congregations, languages, nationalities and professions.

To draw an accurate picture of every part of this international network over seven centuries seems impossible: it would probably require an Encyclopedia as large as the *Britannica*. But a modest outline can be given, and with it some characteristics that seem to be common.

Posing the Questions

Even with this rough preamble, it should be clear that making generalized statements about "Franciscans" is dangerous. To answer the question, "Who are they?" we may say that they are a heterogeneous collection of individuals, united (and divided) by their history.

They are men and women; they are lay and religious. Some are parents, others are priests. There are manual laborers and university professors in their ranks. They live in nearly every nation on earth. Through the first four chapters of this book many individual Franciscans and groups of Franciscans will be described, and the reader will be able to glimpse some of the reasons for the variety that characterizes the membership of the Franciscan family from its very beginnings.

"How did they start?" In answer to this question, the history of the family will be told, describing the soil out of which the family sprouted. We will first examine the lives of Francis and Clare, the two saints whose lives gave birth to today's worldwide Franciscan movement.

"How did they grow?" To understand the growth of this movement, we need to examine a complex story of expansion, reform, division, decline and renewal spanning nearly eight centuries. Not every branch of the family tree can be described here, nor even some very significant figures. To introduce the family to readers who are not among its members, a summary of important movements and moments of this history will provide a "telescopic" view of millions of individuals, in hundreds of independent groupings, in various countries over many centuries. Because of the variety of people who belong to the Franciscan family, it is difficult to respond to the question, "What do they do?" The couple in California work at harvesting, raising their children, keeping a home. They pray at home, meet their brothers and sisters of the Secular Franciscan Order; they participate in the life of their parish, their town. The religious delegates in Manila represent many different communities of Franciscan sisters. One works as an X-ray technician, two serve as organizers of base-communities in a diocese, another is a theology professor. Of the generals meeting in Rome, one has worked as a parish priest for years, one has spent many years teaching in a seminary. The sister in Malawi tends a large garden, celebrates the Divine Office in choir, and prays silently during the long day.

Perhaps the simplest answer to the question would be, "Franciscans do just about everything." But that answer is not very satisfying. A better answer would be, "Let me tell you about some of these people and what they have done." Through the pages of this book, many different activities of Franciscans through the years will be sketched, from the care of lepers to modern psychiatry. These "snapshots" cannot capture all their activities, but can at least indicate that Franciscans do not consider that a particular work defines who they are.

"What do they believe?" They hold similar beliefs about people, God, the world, and the life of the Church, though they may not publicize those beliefs or even make them explicit. In the fifth chapter, I will suggest a vision that underlies many of these beliefs, a "Franciscan theology." In some sense this is the heart of the book, the place where the strands of diversity are woven together in a kind of tapestry of the Franciscan vision of God, people, the world, Christ. I believe that this vision is, ultimately, what holds together the sometimes chaotic diversity of the family, and keeps it alive.

"Where are they today'?" At the end of the book this question will be addressed. The answer will not concern their geographical location, but their "spiritual location." In the last twenty years a deeply spiritual process of renewal within the various branches of the Franciscan family has led to a growing awareness of our common origins, our mutual interdependence, and our shared vision of a life according to the Gospel of Christ. This awareness inspired my efforts to write this book in the way I have written it, to present a picture of a single family, united by its members' struggle to live according to that vision.

1

The Founders:
Francis and Clare[1]

Francis was born in 1182 in Assisi. When he was five years old, Jerusalem fell to the Islamic forces under their leader, Saladin, setting off the enormous enterprise of the Crusades in the Christian West, a movement which would come to influence Francis' life directly, and which had profound consequences for the development of the Franciscan family. By 1189 Francis may have begun his education under the tutelage of the priest at the Church of San Giorgio in Assisi, a place later to be honored

---

1   Abundant historical and biographical materials concerning Francis and Clare are available. Space permits only the mention of a few general works here. Arnaldo Fortini's masterful multi-volume *Nova vita di s. Francesco* (Assisi: 1959) gives extensive background information. English translation by H. Moak, Francis of Assisi (New York: Crossroad, 1981) is a condensed version of the original For early, original sources in English translation, see Regis J. Armstrong OFM Cap., J.A. Wayne Hellmann OFM Conv., William J. Short OFM, eds., *Francis of Assisi: Early Documents*, 3 vols., (Hyde Park, NY: New City Press, 1999-2001), (hereafter *FA:ED*); Regis J. Armstrong OFM Cap., *The Lady: Clare of Assisi: Early Documents* (Hyde Park, NY: New City Press, 2006), (hereafter *CA:ED*). Among the many modern biographies of Francis we may simply note those by such authors as Johannes Jorgensen, G.K. Chesterton, Omer Engelbert, and Julien Green The recent and reliable English edition of the writings of Francis and Clare may be found in Regis Armstrong OFMCap, and Ignatius Brady, OFM, trans. and intro., *Francis and Clare: The Complete Works* (Ramsey, N.J.: Paulist Press, 1982), hereafter, Armstrong-Brady.

by receiving Francis' body at the time of his death, and today incorporated into the beautiful Basilica of St. Clare, whose body rests there today.

Clare was born in the same town of Assisi in 1194, when Francis was eleven years old.[2] The same year saw the birth of the future Holy Roman Emperor Frederick II, who was baptized later in Assisi. Another year passed, and Francis would have begun, at the age of thirteen, to work in his father's business, that of the cloth merchants. When he was sixteen, in 1198, the *Rocca Maggiore,* the fortress of the feudal nobility above Assisi, was attacked by the members of the commune, an act leading to a civil war in Assisi. It set the members of the old nobility against the newly powerful members of the rising merchant class, the two sides represented by the families of Clare, on the one hand, and Francis on the other.

The tides of war moved outward four years later as the commune of Assisi went to war against its archenemy, the hated city of Perugia, its neighbor across the valley. Francis, twenty years old in 1202, participated in the opening battle: the *Assisiani* were roundly beaten, and Francis was taken, a humiliated prisoner, to Perugia. In the following year he was released from prison and returned to Assisi suffering from a serious illness contracted during his imprisonment. The year 1204 saw Francis recovering from his illness and taking up once again his normal duties in his father's business. But Francis did not remain long in Assisi: the next year saw him on his way to the south of Italy, to join another military expedition, this time among the troops of Walter of Brienne, a famous and dashing military commander. Francis

---

2   Some suggest 1193 as the date of Clare's birth. See A. Blasucci, "Chiara d'Assisi," in *Dizionario degli Istituti di Perfezione* (hereafter *DIP*) II (Rome: Edizioni Paoline, 1975) col. 885.

travelled only the short distance from Assisi to Spoleto, just down the valley, before succumbing to illness again. His biographers tell of a vision Francis had at that moment of new disappointment. He saw a hall filled with military weapons and heard a voice asking him, "Is it better to serve the lord or the servant?" Francis responded, "The lord, of course." The voice replied, "Then why do you serve the servant?" Already we begin to notice a change in Francis who now begins to search for the fulfillment of his dreams of knightly glory in a different way.

He returned to Assisi and seemed to be undergoing a religious conversion. He began to seek out solitary places, say early authors, and within a year travelled to Rome as a pilgrim. There, according to his biographer, Thomas of Celano, he mingled with the beggars at the door of the Church of St. Peter, and exchanged his clothes for theirs. On returning to Assisi, he sought a new home with the priest at a run-down little church, San Damiano, outside the town. He made a definitive and painful break with his family and the world of business in which he had earlier worked. Taking cloth from his father's store, he rode to Foligno where he sold the cloth and the horse he was riding in order to raise money to restore the church which hosted him. The year was 1206, and Francis was now twenty-four.

His father had him denounced as a thief and appealed for justice. Since Francis had begun to live as a layman under the protection of the Church, the bishop of Assisi, Guido, convoked father and son to hear the charges and pass judgment at his own court. Francis repudiated his father, giving back to him even the clothes he was wearing, and declared, according to early stories, that now he would call no one "father" except God. He had made a dramatic step toward embracing a new kind of life.

Toward the end of his life Francis himself would speak of the change occurring within him in those early days of new directions. It happened when he was with some lepers. He wrote in his *Testament*:

> The Lord granted me, Brother Francis, to begin to do penance in this way: While I was in sin, it seemed very bitter to me to see lepers. And the Lord Himself led me among them and I had mercy upon them. And when I left them that which seemed bitter to me was changed into sweetness of soul and body; and afterward I lingered a little and left the world.[3]

Francis gave few further indications of what happened during that time: "I left the world." Francis' rough Latin in his *Testament* does not reveal the details. He just "left"— he left the ordinary way of living he knew until then, "the world," as he calls it.

Once again we are left to fill in the details from the stories that were recorded after his death. From these we gather that Francis lived as a kind of lay hermit for a time, and soon identified himself as a "penitent.[4]

The Penitents were members of a widely diffused movement for renewal of Christian life spread throughout Europe in the previous centuries.[5] In Francis' time many lived in or around the fast-growing towns; others lived in more remote areas in the hills or forests. These were men and women who did not belong to the

---

3   Armstrong-Brady, p. 154.

4   On Francis and the Penitents, the most complete study available is Raffaele Pazzelli, *San Francesco e il Terz'Ordine: Il movimento penitenziale pre-francescano e francescano* (Padua Edizioni Messaggero, 1982).

5   For a survey of the penitential movement from the times of the early Church until Francis, see Pazzelli, pp. 39-126.

mainline religious orders. They were lay people from different levels of society who shared a desire to live according to the Gospel as they understood it: giving up property, dedicating themselves to prayer and fasting, working for their sustenance, sometimes preaching. Some lived in communities, some were solitaries. Within this broad movement, Francis chooses a way of living: praying, fasting and working on the repair of small chapels in the countryside near Assisi. Besides the chapel of San Damiano, he also worked at restoring two others whose names are mentioned in early sources: San Pietro, and "the Little Portion," *Porziuncola*, dedicated to St. Mary of the Angels, on the valley floor below Assisi.

These early years of Francis' new "penitent's life" are not described in detail by his later followers. For two or three years he continued to work, finding consolation among lepers, and praying. At the chapel of the *Porziuncola* he heard the Gospel read in which Jesus sends his disciples on their mission, and Francis, on hearing it, decided that his life was to imitate theirs: he gave away his tunic, staff and belt. He would live as the earliest followers of Jesus lived.

The story is one of a change from one way of living to another, the picture of a religious conversion in a man. But this is not yet the story of the large Franciscan Family. It is the story of one person, and could well have remained that.

In 1208 his way of life changed fundamentally: it attracted others who wished to join him in this life. To describe this turning point, Francis wrote in his *Testament* the simple phrase: "the Lord gave me brothers."[6] We know the names of three who would later tell the stories of these early days of a new family. They were

6   Armstrong-Brady, p. 154.

Bernard of Quintavalle, a wealthy citizen of Assisi; Peter Cattaneo (Catanii), a lawyer; and Giles, an illiterate layman with a great gift of prayer. Francis' personal conversion was now part of a common project of life; the Franciscan family was beginning.

They set out on preaching tours in the surrounding areas: to the Marches of Ancona, in the hilly country northeast of their native Umbria; through the Valley of Rieti to the south; to Florence in Tuscany to the north. By 1209 twelve brothers formed the family, and the small band set out for Rome seeking an approval of their "form of life" (*forma vitae*) from the Pope, Innocent III. Francis wrote many years later in his *Testament*:

> And after the Lord gave me brothers, no one showed me what I should do, but the Most High Himself revealed to me that I should live according to the form of the Holy Gospel. And I had this written down simply and in a few words and the Lord Pope confirmed it for me.[7]

The approval was a verbal one, but it satisfied the newly-formed group: they could live under the protection of the Church without fearing the suspicion of heresy attached to some renewal groups of the day.

On their return to Assisi, the small band took up residence in an abandoned building in the valley in the vicinity of the *Porziuncola* chapel. Evicted from this shelter by a local resident, they were permitted to take up residence at the *Porziuncola* by its owners, the monks of the monastery of Mt. Subasio, above the town.

Some scholars suggest that at this time Francis, now twenty-

---

7   *Ibid.*, pp. 154-155.

seven years old, began to guide a larger group of penitents in the area, and wrote for them his "Exhortation to the Brothers and Sisters of Penance." [8] Francis had described his own conversion as "beginning to do penance," and showed for the rest of his life a keen interest in the Order of Penitents, many of whose members associated themselves with his Assisian family. They formed an important part of the Franciscan Movement from its very beginnings. Francis and his brothers even called themselves at first simply Penitents from Assisi, later choosing the name Lesser Brothers (*fratres minores*, or "friars minor").[9]

For the next two years the early sources give us little information about the life of this small group. We know that others joined the group, and we may presume that they continued the kind of life Francis had earlier lived: praying, working on church repair and in other kinds of manual labor, serving among the lepers, begging for their bread when they received no compensation for their work since they had no properties to produce income. Francis had received permission to preach and, during the Lent of 1212 (or 1211) spoke at the Cathedral of San Rufino in Assisi. His words had a profound effect on a young noblewoman who heard them.[10]

At the age of eighteen Lady Chiara, daughter of Sir Favarone di Offreduccio and Lady Ortolana, chose to follow the "life of the Gospel" practiced and preached by Francis and his followers. She made her decision during that Lent, leaving her family's home the night of Palm Sunday, accompanied by "honest company." They

8   Also known as the "short version" or the "first version" of the "Letter to the Faithful," which K. Esser dates to this period. See Armstrong-Brady, pp. 62-65.

9   Pazzelli, p. 226.

10   The possible dates for Clare's decision are given in Blasucci, col. 886.

travelled the few miles from the town to the little church of St. Mary of the Angels in the fields below Assisi. There Francis and his companions, including Rufino and Sylvester, relatives of Clare, received her. Francis cut her hair and dressed her in a plain tunic, marking her as being under the protection of the Church. She went immediately to stay at the women's Benedictine community at nearby Bastia. After "a few days" she moved to the community of women penitents, *bizzocche*, at Sant 'Angelo in Panzo, where her sister Agnes joined her two weeks later. She was not entirely at ease there says Thomas of Celano in his *Life* of Clare, and Francis arranged for her to stay at the chapel of San Damiano, where he had lived and worked on its repair.[11]

Meanwhile other women had come to join Clare at San Damiano, forming a group marked by prayer, by manual labor, and poverty, holding no revenue-producing properties for their upkeep, but having recourse to the "table of the Lord" (begging) when they could not provide for their needs. Sometimes they were called Poor Ladies, Lesser Sisters, or "the poor recluses of San Damiano." Although they were referred to as nuns (*moniales*) in some documents, Clare herself always preferred to call members of her family simply "sisters," and her Order, that of the Poor Sisters.[12] She chose a name that signified their novelty: they were contemplative women who lived an enclosed life with a deep experience of sisterhood but without fixed income.

The winds of religious renewal blowing throughout Europe led Pope Innocent III to call the Fourth Lateran Council in 1215. One of its purposes was to regularize the situation of many different groups who wished to live a more radical form of Christian life,

---

11   I. Omaechevarria, "Clarisse," in *DIP* 11, col 1116.

12   *Ibid.*, col. 1117.

groups dedicated to reform of their own lives and that of the Church at large. The newly-founded groups in Assisi, organized around Francis and Clare, were among the groups under scrutiny. The Council forbad the approval of any new *Rules* for religious groups: all were to accept one of the standard, approved *Rules*, e.g., that of the Benedictines, Cistercians, or Augustinian canons. It was in 1215 that Clare was named "Abbess"[13] of the monastery of San Damiano, a title she did not relish. Probably in 1216 or 1217 Francis composed for her a "form of life" (*forma vitae*) just as he had composed one for his brothers earlier. During these same years Clare received from the Pope the promise of a "privilege of poverty."[14] By this unusual papal favor, she was to be assured that she and her sisters would not be required to own property that would provide them with a fixed source of income (rents from buildings or the sale of crops from land worked by tenant-farmers). Yet in 1219 a *Rule*, composed by Cardinal Ugolino, was approved by Pope Honorius III which gave Clare and her community the *Rule of St. Benedict* as the foundation of their life.

For the next forty years Clare would struggle to gain papal approval for her "form of life" and a *Rule* for her sisters, one which would show them clearly to be members of the Franciscan rather than the Benedictine family of religious. (She would later win her case when the *Rule* she wrote was approved shortly before her death.)

Francis and his brothers were allowed to continue living according to their "form of life," apparently because they had already received verbal approval for it six years before the Council met. The official recognition of their *Rule* would have to wait until

---

13   Blasucci, col. 886.

14   *Ibid.*

1223, but at least they were not required to choose another. This point would eventually help Clare in her efforts to gain approval for her own *Rule* for the Poor Sisters, identical in many places to that of Francis and the Lesser Brothers.

Following the Council, Francis composed a longer version of the "form of life" he had previously given to the Brothers and Sisters of Penance. This is generally known today as the later version of "The Letter to All the Faithful," and outlines the features of the Penitents' life within the orbit of the Assisian movement with careful attention to the concerns of the Council about the dangers of heretical influences in the evangelical movements of the day.[15]

Francis faced a deeply personal question of direction at this time. Drawn to a life of solitude and prayer, but also an effective preacher, he turned to Clare and to Sylvester asking for their help as he tried to discern God's call. Should he pray or should he preach? Their answer was firm: he was to continue on the way he had begun, continuing his work of preaching penance.

That ministry of preaching was to take Francis far from his original home in the countryside around Assisi. The assembly of the brothers (called the General Chapter) in 1217 had sent brother Giles to Tunis, Elias to Syria, and Francis to *Francia* (probably meaning part of today's Belgium). Francis himself was turned back at Florence by the persuasion of Cardinal Ugolino, his advisor and protector of the early Franciscan movement. In 1219 Francis set out on a journey to the Near East, a region convulsed by the war between Christian Crusaders and Islamic forces. With his travelling companion, Brother Illuminato, Francis travelled to meet the Islamic Sultan near the battlefield at Damietta in Egypt.

15   Text in Armstrong-Brady, pp. 66-73. On its importance see Pazzelli, p. 224.

The two unarmed men crossed the no man's land between the camps of the Crusaders and the Islamic army and reached the Sultan. A witness to the events described them in this way:

> We have seen the founder and the master of this Order... he was a simple unlettered man, beloved by God and men; he was called Brother Francis. Spiritual fervor and ecstasy moved him to such excesses that, having arrived at the army of the Christians before Damietta in Egypt, with no fear whatsoever, fortified solely with the 'shield of faith,' he set out for the camp of the Sultan of Egypt. When the Saracens took him prisoner, he said: "I am a Christian! Lead me to your lord!" On seeing the man of God, the Sultan, that cruel beast, became sweetness itself, kept him with him for a few days and with a great deal of attention listened to him preach the faith of Christ to him and to his followers. But in the end he was afraid of seeing some of his soldiers, whom the effective words of this man would have converted to the Lord, go over to the army of the Christians. He, therefore, had Francis led back to our camp with many signs of honor and with safe conduct, but not without saying to him: "Pray for me, that God may reveal to me the law and the faith that is the more pleasing to Him." [16]

Francis returned to Assisi the next year, gravely disturbed by some changes made in the life of the brotherhood during his absence. It was perhaps at this time (if not before his journey) that

16 Jacques de Vitry, *Historia orientalis*, Ch. 32, in Executive Committee of the Franciscan International Mission Council, *Correspondence Course on Franciscan Missionary Charism* (Bonn: Missionzentrale der Franziskaner, 1987) (hereafter. *Charism*) 4:4 and 20:6. U.S. edition: *Build with Living Stones: A Program of Study on the Franciscan Missionary Charism* (Pittsburgh: Franciscan Federation, distributors).

he resigned his office as Minister General of the brothers, and named Peter Cattaneo, an early companion, and a lawyer, as his successor. Peter died shortly afterward, and Elias Bombarone was named to succeed him as Minister General.

During the regular meeting of the brothers' Chapter in 1221, at Pentecost, Francis presented the revised and expanded *Rule* which, until now, had received only verbal approval from the papacy. The *Rule* was not officially accepted, and Francis returned to the task of revising it.[17]

During the year 1222 Francis returned to the work of preaching in southern Italy and later in Bologna in the north. He continued his work of revising the *Rule* of the Lesser Brothers and completed it by 1223. It was confirmed by Honorius III in the fall of that year and has remained, to this day, the *Rule* of the brothers. Having seen the *Rule* approved, Francis attended the Chapter meeting at Pentecost in 1224, the last he was to attend. In September of that year, during a time of retreat at the mountain of La Verna in Tuscany, Francis underwent a profound mystical experience of the crucified Christ, returning from the mountain with the stigmata, the marks of Christ's wounds, in his hands, feet and side.

Francis was already approaching death, worn out by physical austerities and illness. He was nearly blind from eye-disease, and one doctor after another tried to treat him at Assisi itself, at Fonte Colombo, and finally in Siena but without result.

It was during this time of intense physical suffering and near blindness that Francis composed his spiritual masterpiece, *The Canticle of Brother Sun*. A hymn to God's goodness, and the goodness of all creation, it also speaks of impending death:

---

17 On the importance of Cardinal Ugolino in the development of the *Rule* see Pazzelli, p. 234.

Most High, all-powerful, good Lord,

Yours are the praises, the glory, the honor, and all blessing.

To You alone, Most High, do they belong,

and no man is worthy to mention Your name.

Praised be You, my Lord, with all your creatures, especially Sir Brother Sun,

Who is the day and through whom You give us light.

And he is beautiful and radiant with great splendor;

and bears a likeness of You, Most High One.

Praised be You, my Lord, through Sister Moon and the stars,

in heaven You formed them clear and precious and beautiful.

Praised be You, my Lord, through Brother Wind,

and through the air, cloudy and serene, and every kind of weather through which You give sustenance to Your creatures.

Praised be You, my Lord, through Sister Water,

which is very useful and humble and precious and chaste.

Praised be You, my Lord, through Brother Fire,

through whom You light the night

and he is beautiful and playful and robust and strong.

Praised be You, my Lord, through our Sister Mother Earth,

who sustains and governs us,

and who produces varied fruits with colored flowers and herbs.

Praised be You, my Lord, through those who give pardon

for Your love

and bear infirmity and tribulations.

Blessed are those who endure in peace

for by You, Most High, they shall be crowned.

Praised be You, my Lord, through our Sister Bodily Death,

from whom no living man can escape.

Woe to those who die in mortal sin.

Blessed are those whom death will find in

Your most holy will, for the second death shall do them no harm.

Praise and bless my Lord and give Him thanks,

and serve Him with great humility.[18]

On the evening of October 3, 1226, Francis died at the Porziuncola. His body was carried up to the city for burial, first in the Church of San Giorgio (later in the magnificent Basilica built in his honor). On the way to the town gates the procession carrying the dead "little poor man" stopped at the monastery of San Damiano. There Clare and her sisters saw for the last time their brother and their friend, now marked with signs of Christ's wounds.[19]

In 1228 Francis was canonized in Assisi by the former Cardinal Ugolino, now Pope Gregory IX. The new Pope also reconfirmed for Clare the "privilege of poverty," affirming for her and her sisters at San Damiano their right to live without revenues from land holdings or rents from property, but to live by the work of their hands and by begging. Raynald of Segni, papal representative to the communities of Damianite women, listed twenty-five communities of Poor Sisters at this time. Within two years Agnes, Clare's sister, set out from San Damiano to found a new community of Poor Sisters at Monticelli, near Florence. Still Clare had not received official approval of her *Rule*.

Clare's health also began to fail, and she was confined more and more to her sick bed. She suffered new disappointments in her attempts to convince the papacy to approve her *Rule* during

---

18   Armstrong-Brady, pp. 38-39.

19   Blasucci col. 887.

these years. In 1243 Pope Innocent IV refused her request for such approval and reaffirmed the *Rule* issued earlier by his predecessor, Gregory IX. Clare's struggle for the approval of her *Rule* continued for another decade. Innocent IV did, however, allow Clare to win one important point. In 1247, having failed in an attempt to unite the Lesser Brothers and Poor Sisters into one body, the Pope replaced the *Rule* of St. Benedict with that of Francis as the canonical basis for the life of Clare and her sisters. This Clare could consider at least a partial victory in her quest for a *Rule* of her own. While mitigating some of the austerities practiced by the Poor Sisters, the legislation of Innocent IV now recognized the Poor Sisters as belonging officially to the Franciscan, rather than the Benedictine, family.

In the next years Raynald of Segni, Cardinal Protector of the Poor Sisters, proved himself to be Clare's ally, approving, in his role as Protector, the draft of the *Rule* she had composed. In her last year, Clare, on her death bed, received definitive approval of her *Rule* for the community of San Damiano, approval contained in a Bull of Innocent IV given to her on August 9, 1253. She kissed the document as she received it, and died two days later, on August 11, having received at last the approval of the special way of life she had sought for nearly forty years. Hers was the first approved *Rule* written by a woman.

Within two years Clare was officially canonized. The regulations demanding testimony from witnesses in an official papal canonization process have given us an invaluable document of memories regarding Clare from her contemporaries, relatives, and closest companions. The documents of the "Process of Canonization" continue to provide some of our most personal glimpses into the life of this admirable religious leader.[20]

From the time of her canonization the Poor Ladies or Poor Sisters came to be known commonly as the Order of Saint Clare, from which we derive our common English name for them, the Poor Clares.[21]

Clare had outlived Francis by nearly three decades and represented one of the last living witnesses of the early life of the Franciscan family, one to whom many of the brothers had turned for advice and information. With her death, the brothers' direct link with their beginnings was weakened, and within a few years their differences had reached a point of explosive confrontation. Francis and Clare, the founders of the Franciscan Family, had seen its three branches flourish during their lifetimes. The Brothers and Sisters of Penance, the Poor Sisters and the Lesser Brothers were now to follow new leaders and new directions, posing to a new generation the question, "How are we to live the life of the Holy Gospel?"

Early Growth of the Three Orders[22]

---

20 Though the Latin original is lost, a fifteenth-century Italian version of the *Process* has survived, ed. Z. Lazzeri, in *Archivum Franciscanum Historicum* 13 (1920), pp. 403-507. An English translation with notes and commentary has been prepared by the Capuchin Franciscan scholar, Regis Armstrong, and published in his *CA:ED*, pp. 277-329.

21 On the different names for Clare's followers, see E. Frascadore and G. Odoardi, "Francescane, monache," in *DIP* IV (Rome: Edizioni Paoline, 1977) col. 174.

22 For Franciscan history, the most comprehensive treatment available is Lázaro Iriarte, *Fraciscan History: The Three Orders of St. Francis of Assisi*, (Chicago: Franciscan Herald Press, 1982), a translation from the first Spanish edition by Patricia Ross. The results of Iriarte's panoramic study of Franciscan history are condensed and summarized here. A second work from which I have derived much historical material is Damien Vorreux, "Les Franciscains," in *Les Ordres Religieux: La Vie et l'Art*, vol 2: *Les Ordres Actifs*, ed. Gabriel Le Bras (Paris: Flammarion, 1980). pp. 226-373.

During the year following the Fourth Lateran Council of 1215, the French bishop, Jacques de Vitry, visited the Assisi area and noted in his chronicles the admirable life lived by Clare, Francis and the Penitents:

> …a great number of men and women who renounced all their possessions and left the world for the love of Christ 'Friars Minor' and 'Sisters Minor,' as they are called. They are held in great esteem by the Lord Pope and the cardinals. They are totally detached from temporal things and have but one passion to which they devote all their efforts: to snatch from the vanities of the world souls that are in danger and to prevail upon them to imitate their example. Thanks to God, they have already achieved important successes and made numerous conquests. Those who have heard them, say to their friends: "Come along!" and so one group brings another. As for the brothers themselves, they live the life of the primitive Church of which it is written: "The whole group of believers was united, heart and soul."
> During the day they go into the cities and the villages, giving themselves over to the active life of the apostolate; at night, they return to their hermitage or withdraw into solitude to live the contemplative life. (The women) live near the cities in various hospices and refuges; they live a community life supported by the work of their hands, but accept no income. The veneration that the clergy and the laity show towards them is a burden to them and it chagrins and annoys them. Once a year, in a place on which they agree, the men of this Order assemble to rejoice in the Lord and eat together; and they profit greatly from these gatherings. They seek the counsel of upright and virtuous men; they draw up and promulgate holy laws and submit them for

approval to the Holy Father; then they disband again for a year and go about through Lombardy, Tuscany, Apulia, and Sicily. [23]

This picture of the Franciscan Family, as recorded by a contemporary, shows its very early days. Francis had begun his life as a penitent about ten years earlier. The Lesser Brothers, or Friars Minor had only existed for about five years. Clare and the Poor Sisters (or Sisters Minor, as Jacques de Vitry writes) were only three or four years old.

In the following pages we will see how the various parts of the family grew during the decades following the French bishop's visit to the region of Assisi. While connected with the stories of Francis and Clare, the Franciscan Family's history will show that the founders themselves were not always the only, or even the most important influences shaping the new movement.

The Brothers and Sisters of Penance

During the five years that followed Jacques de Vitry's 1216 visit, the Brothers and Sisters of Penance were being organized in a more formal way. Probably under the direction of Cardinal Ugolino, an official *Rule* for the Penitents was drawn up in 1221, known as the *Memoriale propositi*, whose original has not come down to us. The reigning pope, Honorius III, extended his influence to protect the Penitents, sending a Bull to the bishop of Rimini urging the protection of the Penitents against the civic authorities who were trying to force them to take up arms, under oath, to protect the city.[24]

---

23 Jacques de Vitry, *Lettres de Jacques de Vitry*: Edition critique (Leiden: 1960) Lettre I, in *Charism* 5:5.

24 On their freedom from oaths to protect rulers, see Iriarte, p. 480.

During the five years following John Parenti's election as Minister General in 1227, his direction led the brothers to take an active role in promoting the life and organization of the Brothers and Sisters of Penance. Within a year the Penitents had a version of their *Rule*, still existing today, called the *Capestrano Rule*, after the town where it was kept.

During the seven years following his election as Minister General in 1232, Elias Bombarone rejected the claim that the Lesser Brothers should take responsibility for the direction of the Brothers and Sisters of Penance. This issue of responsibility for the Penitents, like that of their responsibility for communities of Poor Sisters, was destined to change with almost every change in the leadership of the Lesser Brothers as the papacy insisted and the brothers temporized.

The Minister General in 1247, John of Parma, received a papal Bull enjoining the ministers of the Lesser Brothers in Italy and Sicily to provide for the permanent visitation of the Brothers and Sisters of Penance. Yet soon afterward, at least in northern Italy, different arrangements were decided: John directed that the fraternities of Penitents in Lombardy and Florence were to be under the control of the local bishop.

The Minister General elected in 1257, Bonaventure of Bagnoregio, opposed any commitment of the Lesser Brothers' energies to directing the Brothers and Sisters of Penance. A document published at this time, though probably not his, listed the many reasons for which such a commitment was incompatible with the life of the Lesser Brothers.

New legislation was also developing for the Brothers and Sisters of Penance. By 1284 the legal connections between the Penitents and the Lesser Brothers were strengthened. Brother

Caro of Florence, "Apostolic Visitor" of the Penitents, composed a *Rule* for their life. Within five years, Pope Nicholas IV used this document as the basis for his Bull (*Supra montem*) promulgating the *Rule* for "all present and future Brothers and Sisters of Penance." The Bull retains almost every element of the so-called *Capestrano Rule*, while rearranging its parts. He officially named Saint Francis as the founder of the order of Penitents, and decreed that all the *visitatores* and *informatores* (we might say, "councillors and inspectors") were to be from the Order of the Lesser Brothers, under whose authority the Penitents were to live. While some of the Penitents opposed this move, these papal decisions remained in force for six centuries until the pontificate of Leo XIII at the end of the nineteenth century.[25]

The Poor Sisters

While all the branches of the Assisi Family were growing, Cardinal Ugolino, advisor and protector of the family, was organizing new women's communities along lines similar to those of the San Damiano community. Ugolino sent his chaplain, Ambrose, a Cistercian monk, to San Damiano where a new, stricter form of enclosure (cloister) was applied, as had been applied in the previous decade to Cistercian nuns.

A papal bull of 1227 made the care of the Poor Sisters the responsibility of the Lesser Brothers. Small groups of brothers were to be attached to each monastery of the Poor Sisters, brothers exempted from ordinary observance and from apostolic tasks. This arrangement would later be criticized, and the brothers at various times would attempt to avoid this responsibility.

The Poor Sisters continued their steady growth in the years

---

25   *Ibid.*, p. 478

following Francis' death and began to expand beyond Italy. Princess Agnes of Bohemia, refusing the offer of a dynastic marriage, chose to embrace the life of the Poor Sisters, founding a community in Prague. She corresponded with Clare about her intentions and her project, and Clare's letters to Agnes have been preserved for us, giving us a priceless collection of documents revealing the spirituality and personality of the leader of the Damianite women.

Though Clare was cheered by the news of Agnes' decision, she had continuing difficulties over the issue of the *Rule* to be followed at San Damiano. In 1238 she tried to receive approval for her own *Rule* from Pope Gregory IX, but he refused. The same Pope, also impressed with the decision of Agnes to join the family of the Poor Sisters, wrote to her mentioning the "three orders" founded by Francis: the lesser brothers, the enclosed sisters, and the penitents. It is the first document we have which mentions the "three orders" of St. Francis.[26]

Crescentius of Iesi, elected Minister General of the Lesser Brothers in 1243, forbad his brothers to assume responsibility for the care of the communities of Poor Sisters.

Innocent IV did not approve Clare's *Rule* in 1243 as she had hoped, but he did try to strengthen the bonds between the Poor Sisters and the Lesser Brothers. He issued two Bulls insisting that the sisters should be entirely under the guidance and control of the brothers, and attempted to amalgamate the Poor Sisters to the Order of the Lesser Brothers. In 1247 a Chapter met in France, at Lyon, and elected brother John of Parma as Minister General, and reaction there against the proposed amalgamation of Lesser Brothers and Poor Sisters led the Pope to revise his position.

---

26   *Ibid.*, Clare's letters to Agnes are in *CA:ED*, pp. 43-58..

Innocent IV did, however, insist that the Cardinal Protector was no longer to have a say in the sisters' affairs: this role was to be exercised only by the leadership of the brothers who were to have complete authority over the women's monasteries, a responsibility the brothers were usually unwilling to accept.

Within a few years the solution of the Poor Sisters' problems with the Lesser Brothers became urgent. The brothers, despite the Pope's clear instructions, resisted the obligations of caring for the communities of sisters. The Cardinal Protector, Raynald of Segni, gradually reasserted his authority and wrote to the General Chapter in 1250 that the Lesser Brothers were forbidden to interfere in the affairs of the sisters' communities, claiming for himself absolute control of their monasteries.

After Clare's *Rule* was approved shortly before her death in 1253, it was used by few monasteries beyond that of San Damiano. Though following different *Rules*, the Poor Sisters belonged to the same family, and their numbers were growing. The number of communities of Poor Sisters at the time of Clare's death was large, well over a hundred monasteries scattered throughout Europe: sixty-eight in Italy alone, twenty-one in Spain, fourteen in France, eight in Germanic territories.

As Minister General, Bonaventure showed his interest in encouraging the growth of the Poor Sisters, allowing the brothers to undertake the tasks of spiritual assistance to new followers of St. Clare. A new community of Poor Sisters was founded at Longchamp in France in 1259 by Isabel of France, sister of the King, St. Louis. With a new *Rule* (called the *Rule of Longchamp*), Isabel allowed her community to own property and receive perpetual revenues, while taking a special vow of enclosure leading to their being known as "enclosed (cloistered) Lesser

Sisters" (*sorores minores inclusae*). Isabel's *Rule* was later adopted by other communities of women in France, England, and Italy producing a new branch of the family founded by Clare.

Isabel's *Rule* was officially approved by Pope Urban IV in 1263, as he promulgated a new *Rule* for the Poor Sisters generally, officially naming them the Order of Saint Clare. Based in part on the *Rule* Clare had written, this new legislation for the women's communities drew heavily on the *Rule* drawn up by Pope Innocent IV in 1247, the one in which they were officially recognized as Franciscan, rather than Benedictine religious. In these new regulations, Pope Urban released the Lesser Brothers from the obligation to provide for the spiritual assistance of the women's communities. The family of Clare divided further: some following the *Rule* of Clare, others the *Rule* of Pope Urban, a third group following that of Isabel of France.

Though divided according to their observance of different *Rules*, the Poor Sisters flourished and expanded. The first martyrs of the family of Clare died in the monastery of Tripoli at its fall to the Sultan of Egypt in 1289. Two years later, seventy women of the community at Tolemaida were killed during the Islamic invasion there.

By the end of the century the number of communities of Poor Sisters had grown enormously: we know of 413 monasteries under the guidance of ministers of the Lesser Brothers (others were under the authority of the bishops). Of these, 196 were in Italy, 23 in Dalmatia and the Near East, 57 in Spain and Portugal, 68 in France, 46 in Germanic and Slavonic territories, and 23 in the British Isles. By 1371 the number of monasteries affiliated with the Lesser Brothers had grown to 452, very often with large communities, comprising a total perhaps as large as 15,000 Poor

Sisters, without counting many others whose monasteries were within episcopal jurisdictions.

The Lesser Brothers

Three years after Jacques' visit in 1216, the brothers' numbers had increased and the horizon of their activity had expanded. A Chapter meeting was held, at which the brothers decided to go to Islamic countries. One group set out for the Kingdom of Morocco, while Francis and a companion, Brother Illuminato, went to see the Sultan at Damietta in Egypt. During Francis' absence the brothers were led by two vicars, Matthew of Narni and Gregory of Naples. Within a short time the vicars imposed rules of fasting and observances resembling those of monastic communities. A building program began, a study-house was built in Bologna, and a building at the Porziuncola was constructed with funds from the town of Assisi. Other new ventures were undertaken like that of Brother John of Cappella who tried unsuccessfully to organize the lepers with whom he worked into a new order of lepers.

Francis was disturbed by the changes made during his absence. But he was also ill after his year of travel in the Near East with his eyesight failing and his body weakening from his prolonged fasts. During the six years remaining in his life, Francis moved away from the center of the Order's life resigning his office as Minister General. Succeeded briefly by his old companion, Peter Cattaneo, and then by Elias Bombarone, Francis stayed more and more in the hermitages, and worked on revising the *Rule* before its final approval in 1223. By the time of his death in 1226 other leaders had taken command of the fraternity.

Following Francis' death, Thomas of Celano was commissioned to write the *Life* of Francis, a task he completed in time for Francis' canonization in 1228. At the brothers' Chapter meeting at Pentecost of 1227, the minister of the province of Spain, brother John Parenti, was elected Minister General replacing Elias.

During these years immediately following Francis' death, the Lesser Brothers began to struggle over issues which were destined to divide them profoundly. The Chapter of 1230 had to confront serious tensions among the brothers in regard to the *Rule* and its interpretation. A commission appointed to clarify doubtful points received from Gregory IX a Bull (*Quo elongati*) interpreting portions of the *Rule*. The Minister General, John Parenti, resigned in 1232 and, at a Chapter convoked in Rieti, Elias Bombarone was elected as Minister General, a post he had filled earlier during Francis' last years.

Growing discontent with Brother Elias' exercise of the office of Minister General led an English friar, Haymo of Faversham, to lead a campaign to force Elias from his post. A Chapter was called at Rome with Pope Gregory IX presiding. There, the minister of the province of England, Albert of Pisa, was elected. He died within a few months, and Haymo was chosen to replace him. This energetic leader issued the first "Constitutions" or bylaws of the brothers, revealing Haymo's admiration for the style of the friars of the Order of Preachers, the Dominicans. He encouraged the move away from small country places and into larger urban "convents" or religious houses. He strengthened the role of study in the training of new recruits and encouraged forms of regular or monastic observance and customs. Begging was emphasized, with less emphasis on manual labor, and a strong clericalizing tendency grew in importance.

These issues of social location, style of observance and customs, study, and clerical character, were destined to mark the brothers' life with painful divisions in the centuries to follow.

The rift was already visible by 1241, fifteen years after Francis' death. A "Chapter of Definitors," or councillors, was called, and commissions were established in each region (province) to settle doubtful points about the Rule's interpretation. The issues are clearly presented in one document from this time, *Expositio quattuor magistrorum*, an "exposition" or explanation of the Rule developed by four "masters," university-trained brothers.

Haymo of Faversham died in 1243, and Crescentius of Iesi succeeded him as Minister General. He instructed Thomas of Celano to compose a new *Life* of Francis, drawing on materials not previously compiled. The result, the *Rememberance* or *Second Life*, preserved memories of Francis from his earliest companions and remains an important source for our knowledge of Francis today.

In 1255, while Clare was being glorified in the solemn rites of a papal canonization ceremony, all was not well in the ranks of the brothers. Clare's death broke one strong link between the origins of the family and its new members. A conflict broke out soon after her death and may now appear to us as the beginning of a long, sad story of intrafamily feuding. In 1257 a Chapter was called at Rome, with the purpose of deposing the Minister General, John of Parma, considered a partisan of the Spirituals (a party in the Order dedicated to reform) and suspected of dangerous sympathies with the teaching of Joachim of Fiore, an apocalyptic mystic whose theories appealed to the Spirituals. Asked to designate his successor, John named Brother (Saint) Bonaventure of Bagnoregio, a forty year-old Master of Theology teaching at the University of Paris. As Minister General of a divided and expanded Order, Bonaventure moved decisively to contain centrifugal forces of reform and division threatening the unity of the Order.

Fifty years after its founding, the Franciscan Family in its three Orders had grown at an impressive rate. Penitents and Poor Sisters, Lesser Brothers and their respective leaders had transformed the ideal of their founders into an international movement. Those founders had died, and a new generation held the responsibility for taking the movement toward the future. In the following pages we will examine the forces that threatened the Lesser Brothers with division, forces destined to affect all the branches of the family in succeeding generations.

2

The Lesser Brothers
and Their Various Branches

For a meeting of major superiors of the Franciscan Family in 1987, the organizers asked me to prepare a short exposition of the "expression of the Franciscan charism" in the branch of the family to which I belong, the Order of Friars Minor. Basing my reflection on the work I had been doing for this book, I concluded that an appropriate motto might be *ordo sine ordine* or "the Disorder of Friars Minor." Why? Because as soon as order was established among the friars, inevitably, a group expressed their desire for "reform" and a new branch of the family grew.

Since this book is meant to introduce readers to the Franciscans, rather than resolve disputes among specialists, I have chosen to summarize and simplify the complex history of the First Order, the Order of Lesser Brothers. Each of its seven centuries produced at least one reform, and several produced three or four, not all of which can be mentioned here.

The themes of reform and organization may be a help to the non-specialist to understand this history. Simply put, the Franciscan Order has grown in moments of reforming inspiration, like that of its early years. Gradually the inspiration and sense of new adventure become routinized, as the community seeks greater solidity and uniformity. Once that solidity is achieved, some members of the community are dissatisfied—the sense of inspiration and new beginnings is lost. They begin to demand "reform" and embody it in a new community which gradually seeks greater solidity as the cycle of reform and organization continues.

This back-and-forth movement between reform and organization may be called the "Franciscan Dialectic," the dynamic opposition of two tendencies within the Order, one centrifugal, the other centripetal, characteristic of many other groups, even of Christianity itself.

Other terms have been used to describe the two poles of this movement: charism and institution, spirit and law, renewal and decadence. The choice of terms depends on an author's judgment of the value of the two. In every century of Franciscan history, members of the "organization" distrusted the "reformers," often picturing them as selfish and egocentric malcontents who only wished to be different in order to seem more important. "Reformers" usually returned the compliment by accusing members of the "organization" of tepidity, lack of zeal, and abandonment of authentic Franciscan ideals. Both tendencies have had holy and dedicated adherents, many canonized as saints. And both groups have known scandals and abuses, not the least of which was their animosity toward members of the "opposition."

The history of these developments is the story of a scandal, "the scandal of Franciscan history," as it is called by Lázaro Iriarte, the contemporary Capuchin historian of Franciscanism. In the Preface to his work on Franciscan history, a work that has constantly served as a foundation for my own, Iriarte recalls the thought of Agostino Gemelli, a Franciscan psychologist of the 20th century. The internal struggles of the Order reproduce internal contrasts in the life of Francis himself: a severe sense of discipline and a concern for autonomy, a thirst for solitude and the urge toward an apostolate among people, an aspiration to nothingness and a need for action.[1] Quoting the historian of religious orders, L. Moulin, Iriarte continues:

> The order which has been through most crises is certainly that of St. Francis, a fine example of triumphant anarchy… On the human level, it must be admitted that to have emerged victorious from so many crises is at least a sign of extraordinary vitality.[2]

In the pages to follow, both that anarchy and its accompanying vitality will require our attention.

The History of Division

I am writing these words in the Franciscan friary of Monte Mesma, near the Italian-Swiss border. This house sits high on its own hill. To the north is Switzerland, to the south the Piedmont of Italy. To the east is Lombardy; to the west, as I write, the sun is setting behind Monte Rosa in the Alps of the Val d'Aosta. Far below my window is Lake Orta with the tiny Island of San Giulio and its ancient monastery of Benedictine nuns.

Despite its peaceful and beautiful setting, this house holds memories of turbulence and division, the almost continual

---

1   *Il francescanesimo* (Milan: Vita e pensiero, 1936) p. 40, in Iriarte, p. xvi.

2   *Vita e governo degli Ordini religiosi* (Milan: Vita e pensiero, 1965) p. 36, in Iriarte, p. xvi.

splintering and reorganization of Francis' family. In this house, in the quiet of this winter evening, I wish to tell the story of reform in the Franciscan Family, concentrating on the history of the Lesser Brothers. The story is not unique to them—reform and division also touched the Poor Ladies and the Brothers and Sisters of Penance—but the story of the Lesser Brothers illustrates well the dynamics of reform that have influenced many parts of the Franciscan Family.[3]

The friary of Monte Mesma was founded in the seventeenth century as a house for the *riformati*, "reformed" friars. Even their name suggests that divisions had occurred among the Lesser Brothers in the four centuries that separate the founding of Monte Mesma from the founding of the Order.

How did there come to be a group of friars who called themselves "reformed"? They organized in the sixteenth century to promote a more austere and contemplative life among the friars. They shared many of the values that characterized another group, the Friars of the Eremitical Life, known today as the Capuchins. The Capuchins were recognized as an independent branch in 1619, while the "reformed" friars remained within the orbit of the Observant friars, the group that gave rise to both.

But who were the Observants? They were members of an earlier reform that spread through the Order in the fifteenth century. The Observants became a separate body in 1517 when, by papal decree, the Order divided into two independent branches, one called the Observant Friars and the other, the Conventual Friars. These

---

3   The story of succeeding reforms, seen from the perspective of one friary, forms the organizing principle for a delightful and rare study: P. Alessio D'Arquata, *Cronaca della Riformata Provincia de Minori nella Marca* (Cingoli Luchetti, 1893). For example, Spirituals, Observants, Reformed and Capuchins figure in the history of a single friary, now abandoned, that of Il Sasso in Montefalcone Appennino.

three groups, the Conventuals, Capuchins and Observants, still exist today, as three independent religious Orders. Together they make up the three branches of the "first" Order of the Franciscan Family, the Lesser Brothers.

But why did the Order divide at all so that today there are three independent branches of Lesser Brothers? The brothers divided in the early years of the sixteenth century at the time of the Protestant Reformation because of irreconcilable differences about how the *Rule* should be interpreted and lived. The disputes had pitted Observants against Conventuals throughout the fifteenth century. Their disputes, in turn, harkened back to the painful and sometimes violent conflicts between friars sympathetic to the radical positions of the Spiritual party and the friars of the moderate Community party in the fourteenth century.

The friars of the Community and the Spirituals represent two major bodies of opinion inherited from the friars of the thirteenth century, including the contemporaries of Francis himself. In this chapter we will examine briefly the dynamic movement of splintering and regrouping that gave rise to these different groups.

A recent, masterful study entitled *Reform and Division in the Franciscan Order* explains these developments very thoroughly, from the time of Francis through the Capuchin Reform of the Reformation period. I can do no better here than summarize the process as the author, Duncan Nimmo, has described it, without pretending to include in these few pages all the important information his nearly seven-hundred page study presents so well.[4]

---

4   Duncan Nimmo, *Reform and Division in the Medieval Franciscan Order: From Saint Francis to the Foundation of the Capuchins (Bibliotheca Seraphico-Capuccina 33)* (Rome: Capuchin Historical Institute, 1987).

To understand the ways in which the seeds of nearly perpetual reform and division were planted in the very center of the Franciscan Movement, we can focus our attention on a few important features of the "form of life" Francis gave to the Lesser Brothers in his *Rule*.

As Nimmo emphasizes, Chapter Ten of the *Rule* is an odd text to find in a legislative document, the juridical basis for the Order of Friars Minor. In it Francis wrote:

> ...I strictly command them to obey their ministers in all those things which they have promised the Lord to observe and which are not against [their] conscience and our Rule. And wherever there are brothers who know and realize that they cannot observe the Rule spiritually, it is their duty and right to go to the minister for help. The ministers on their part should receive them with great kindness and love...[5]

The text, at first reading, may seem to be unremarkable. The brothers are to be obedient but they should not obey if the minister commands something "unconscionable" or contradictory to the *Rule* all the brothers have vowed to observe.

We have an example of Francis' own handwriting to help us ponder this question further. The "Letter to Brother Leo" is our only autographed letter of the Saint, and there Francis wrote:

> In whatever way it seems best to you to please the Lord God and follow His footprints and His poverty, do this with the blessing of the Lord God and my obedience.[6]

---

5   Armstrong-Brady, p. 143.

6   *Ibid* p. 48.

Francis gave the blessing of obedience to Leo's personal choice of the best way to follow the Lord's "footprints" and his poverty. The command of obedience is, in simple terms, "do what you think best." Obedience here is based on personal liberty, inspired by the desire to please the Lord and follow his example. History shows us that many friars, wishing to follow the Lord's footprints and his poverty and fulfilling the instructions of Chapter Ten of the *Rule* discovered:

—that they could not obey their ministers in conscience and according to the Rule;

—that they could not observe the Rule spiritually in the places where they were;

—and, when they had recourse to their ministers, these did not always receive them kindly.

Hence the dilemma arose: should they obey their ministers against their consciences and the *Rule*, or obey the *Rule* and their consciences, disobeying their ministers and suffering the consequences?

The difficulties may have begun already during Francis' lifetime: they were certainly noticeable shortly after his death. Here we ask, "What provoked the crisis of conscience among the brothers?" To answer this question, we need to examine changes in the life of the brothers: changes of place, of status, and of style. Reaction to these changes led to the profound crisis that began the movements for reform and ultimately produced division in the Order of Friars Minor.

A Change of Place[7]

Early Franciscan settlements were simply called *loci*, "places." These settlements consisted of an abandoned chapel with some temporary shelters around it located outside a town. Some of these, like the Porziuncola near Assisi, were a short walk from town. Others, like the mountain retreat of La Verna, were more isolated. The brothers who lived in the "places" near towns in the early years were described by a contemporary, Jacques de Vitry:

> ...during the day [they] worked in the towns for the salvation of others. At night they retired to their places outside the towns devoting themselves to contemplation.[8]

Their life was "suburban," outside the towns, and consisted of work and prayer.

In the suburban places their day included work in a hospital for lepers near the Porziuncola and in work around their small settlement keeping the garden, cutting wood, and cooking. They worked as domestic servants in private homes (excluding, however, the job of head butler), and they employed their technical skills to provide for their needs. These technical skills were especially important and earned a special chapter in the *Rule* (Chapter Five) where Francis insisted that each brother should develop some skill or trade and have the tools necessary to continue it. The brothers supported themselves ordinarily by their work, accepting as payment whatever they needed except money. When they did not receive enough from their work to provide for necessities, the brothers begged from door to door to "put dinner on the table."

---

7   See Iriarte, pp. 93-98.

8   Letter I (October, 1216), in Iriarte, p. 93.

The stockpiling of provisions for future needs was not allowed.

The brothers also preached. The example of their work and humility was the form of preaching obligatory for all. They also preached in brief exhortations to practice virtue and avoid vice. Some brothers, with the permission of their minister, and after careful examination, might preach formally on matters of doctrine. Their preaching, however, was only to be done with the permission of the local bishop.

The brothers did not usually have a fixed residence. They travelled a good deal, two by two, working and begging to support themselves as they preached in a district. Some even undertook long journeys as missionaries, as Francis himself did in the Middle East.[9]

Standing back somewhat from the center of population were the more remote places like the retreat on the mountain of La Verna in Tuscany. Life there was more contemplative in emphasis though it shared many features of life in the "suburbs." There was the ordinary work of gathering wood on the mountain, maintaining the garden, and cooking. But the brothers here remained "at home" during the day, remaining mostly in silence and prayer, in a typically Franciscan form of the hermits' life. As the number of brothers increased, during Francis' later years and especially in the decade following his death, there was an "urbanizing movement" in the Order. Often at the invitation of city governments, the brothers moved to places inside the towns, into houses offered to them by civic benefactors. Urban churches were also given to them or built for them. The friars began to assume more and more fixed and specifically ecclesiastical duties: celebrating the Office more solemnly in the choirs of their own

---

9   *Ibid.*, p. 94.

churches; the priests celebrating Mass there, preaching sermons, hearing confessions; counseling and advising the faithful; conducting funerals and accepting the offerings of the people for all these services.

The friars' services were soon in great demand: the official Church found in them an orthodox response to urgent needs for the pastoral care of the faithful. The services most in demand were those offered by priests, and the Order responded by selecting more and more priests or candidates for the priesthood as its new members.

A Change of Status

Here two changes were being made simultaneously: a change of place and a change of status, from outside the town to inside and from lay to cleric. The change was rapid, effectively "in place" within ten years of Francis' death, though it had already begun in his last years.[10]

The dual change—urban and priestly—was reinforced by the need for study to prepare new members for the growing ecclesiastical responsibilities of the Order. There had been some "university men" among the early brothers: Peter Cattani, a layman, was a degreed lawyer; Anthony of Padua, a priest, was a Master of Theology. Shortly after Francis' death the friars moved quickly and forcefully into the universites: at Paris, Oxford, and Bologna. The number of student-friars grew dramatically, and study—philosophical and theological— gained recognition as an appropriate "work" of the friars. Manual labor gradually came to be considered unworthy of clerics. Priestly ordination was decided as the rule for all friars; lay friars would only be accepted

---

10   See Lawrence C. Landini, OFM, *The Causes of the Clericalization of the Order of Friars Minor, 1209-1260, in the Light of Early Franciscan Sources* (Chicago: 1968).

with special permission.[11]

The urban character of the clerical change was in its turn reinforced by the program of study. The universities were in urban centers and the friars needed large houses nearby in which to train students. Funds were also needed to feed and house growing numbers of professors and students. Large churches were built to accommodate the throngs of the faithful who attended the friars' sermons and religious functions. The offerings of the faithful, now usually money, soon became the major source of that funding, replacing the earlier practice of relying on the friars' exercise of trades and manual labor as the major sources of support. The earlier practice of begging came to be understood as the organized collection of funds on a large scale for the support of increasingly large and costly institutions.

A Change of Style

These developments together constituted a change in style: from rather small suburban places to larger and permanent "friaries" or "convents" in cities, from a more mobile to a more fixed community, from a strongly accented contemplative life to one dominated by parochial ministry and scholarship, from a community markedly lay in character to one largely clerical, from living by manual labor and some begging to one based more and more on gifts from the faithful for religious services.[12]

It is not surprising that some friars began to contest the "adaptations" and to call for a return to an earlier system of place, of status, and of style. This return to earlier values emphasized the importance of three interrelated issues: the importance of the

---

11   Iriarte, p. 99.

12   *Ibid.,* p. 105.

hermitage, the role of the lay friars, and the observance of authentic poverty. During the next centuries one reform movement after another would repropose the primacy of the contemplative life whose emblem was the hermitage, would offer a greater role to the lay friars, and would insist on a more genuinely poor life for the brothers.

The story of these attempts at reform is often a sad one including intolerance, beatings, imprisonment, even violent death. At a few points it is also a story of great courage, virtue, mutual understanding and of the triumph of brotherly charity. These stories are part of the heritage bequeathed to all contemporary Franciscans, especially to the friars of the First Order. They have determined, for better or worse, who we are today, an Order both reformed and divided.

Knowledge of Origins and Seeds of Discord

Signs of discontent in the Order appeared among some of the Lesser Brothers in Italy as early as the 1230s, just a few years after Francis' death. Friars dissatisfied with the course being taken by the majority called for a return to the early form of life of Francis and his first companions. Some of these early followers were still living and became a point of reference for a "third generation" of friars. These had not known Francis personally. They had been formed in the "second generation," that of expansion and adaptation of the 1220s. They now led the movement for reform, calling for a return to earlier ideals and practices.

One reason for the sharp division of opinion about how to live the Franciscan life lies in different levels of information about Francis and the ideals of the early Order. Within a decade of Francis' death, many friars had little personal knowledge of the origins of the Order. These members of the second and third

Franciscan generations had little contact with the Order's roots, whether through personal acquaintance or literary tradition. For example, a man joining the Order in 1240 in Germany probably had only a vague notion of the primitive Order, its ideals and practices. He was geographically distant from the Order's center at the Porziuncola and probably had no contact with "founding members" of the fraternity.

Francis himself had withdrawn from the Order's leadership during the years of rapid expansion. Nimmo suggests that perhaps as early as the Chapter of 1217 Francis had renounced the office of Minister General. From this early date (or perhaps a few years later) the founder became more distant from the evolving fraternity. In 1219-1220 he was in Egypt and the Near East, returning to Italy to work on the *Rule,* presenting one draft in 1221 and the final draft in 1223. Following the approval of the *Rule,* he was increasingly withdrawn, afflicted with a grave illness and dedicated himself to an intense personal spiritual journey. In Christmas of 1223 he celebrated the feast of the Nativity at the hermitage of Greccio, and in September 1224 he received the Stigmata at La Verna. He spent most of his time in remote hermitages with a few close companions, none of whom was involved, it would seem, in the official administration of the rapidly expanding Order.

During the time of this "second generation," the friars' movement was expanding beyond its original home in Italy. Friars who entered the fraternity in these years had little personal access to Francis and his closest companions. In his last years, 1223-1226, Francis turned from personal visits to writing in order to communicate with others in circular letters, his *Testament,* and in the brief last will he sent to Clare and her sisters. These documents were important to him, and he asked the friars to keep them and copy them. Despite his wishes, these writings remained almost unknown to the great majority of the friars, the Community, in the thirteenth century. The *Testament* in particular was put aside: "…the majority of friars, we may suppose, simply shied away from it as being too hot to handle."[13]

If personal contact with Francis was impossible and knowledge of his writings slight, there remained the biographies as a source of information. The most significant works were those of Thomas of Celano, the *First Life* and the *Rememberance* of Francis, and the *Tract on the Miracles*, three very different works composed over a twenty-year period following Francis' death. The Chapter of 1260 asked Bonaventure to compose a new *Life* and the 1263 Chapter at Pisa approved it, the *Legenda Major or Major Life* of St. Francis. In 1266 at Paris the Chapter decreed the suppression of all previous *Lives*. (Curiously, the 1268 Padua Chapter announced a search for any unknown writings of Francis and the early companions.) Bonaventure's account, while generally accurate, accommodated the portrait of Francis to support views of the Order and its role in the Church as these were conceived in the mid-thirteenth century. For most friars Bonaventure's work, alongside the *Rule*, became the nearly exclusive source of knowledge about the beginnings of the Order.

The Spirituals and Their Sources

The Spirituals as a group intended to recreate the life of Francis and his earliest companions. They were convinced that many of the ways in which the Order had accommodated itself to new circumstances really changed the direction Francis had set. They longed for a return to a more "primitive" observance of

---

13   Nimmo, p. 72.

the *Rule*, and held Francis' *Testament* to be the key to interpreting it. They were in many ways well-equipped to undertake their task of turning the Order back toward its original vision. They were particularly fortunate to be linked to the early days of the Order by both strong bonds of personal contact and by familiarity with an extensive literary tradition largely unknown in the Order at large. They had, as Nimmo illustrates convincingly, greater access to information about the origins of the Order than did the majority of the friars.

If we consider that, while Francis died in 1226, some of his early followers outlived him by half a century, we gain some notion of the possibilities the Spirituals had for personal contact with early companions, their models of inspiration. Bernard of Quintavalle, the first companion, joined Francis in 1209 and lived until 1241. Clare died in 1253. Giles, the third companion, died perhaps as late as 1262. Of the so-called "Three Companions," Francis' closest friends and advisors, it seems that Angelo of Rieti died in 1258, Rufino by 1253 and Leo as late as the early 1270s, more than fifty years after the founder.[14]

These early followers kept in touch with each other, and Clare seems to have been the center of the group until her death. The importance of personal contact in the Spirituals' tradition can be seen in the personal story of Angelo Clareno. He died in 1337, more than a century after Francis. He joined the Order around 1270, more than three decades after Francis' death. Yet he had met Angelo of Rieti and Giles (with his constant companion, Brother John) and perhaps also knew Brother Leo. Though he had no direct personal knowledge of Francis, he knew personally those who were with him from the beginning.

---

14   *Ibid.*, p. 79.

Another example is that of Ubertino da Casale. Born in the late 1250s, he said he was told about Francis by some of the saint's own companions. Not all believe that Ubertino really interviewed the early companions, but he and Angelo did belong to a generation of friars who could have met friars who were a generation older than they. These elder friars shared ideals similar to those of the Spirituals, though they never joined the party. Among these we might mention a man of the stature of John of Parma, Minister General from 1247-1257, preceding Bonaventure. In 1294, during his enforced retirement at the hermitage of Greccio, this old man made a lasting impression on the younger Ubertino who was staying there.[15]

Another personality of this calibre was Conrad of Offida, associated with the region of the Marches of Ancona. A friend of Brother Leo, and a friend of the Spirituals, though not belonging to their group, Conrad kept in touch with Angelo Clareno and Ubertino, handing on stories he received from Brother Leo and other early companions of Francis. James of Massa, also from the Marches, was a great collector of stories of the "early days." He was a friend of Brother Leo, Giles, Clare and two other early companions, Masseo and Simon. He maintained close contact with Conrad of Offida and with Angelo Clareno.

Besides these personal contacts with early companions, the Spirituals also drew on an extensive literary tradition largely unexploited or unknown in the Order at large. They showed familiarity with a very complete corpus of Francis' writings, even mentioning some that are not known to us, perhaps drawing on a collection made by Brother Leo himself. They also drew on rich biographical materials collected in the circle of the companions.

---

15   *Ibid.*, p. 80.

We may conclude from this information, as Nimmo presents it, that the friars who desired a return to an earlier form of life, whether members of the Spirituals' party or simply sympathetic to their ideals, had a level of knowledge about the Order's origins superior to that of the Community, the majority party of the Order. Their greater familiarity with early members of the Order and a wider corpus of Franciscan literature led them to object more and more stridently to changes in the Order's life.

The Papal Declarations

The center of dispute between the Community and the Spirituals was the teaching and example of Francis himself, especially regarding the observance of poverty. In the years immediately following Francis' death this observance had been mitigated by papal decrees meant to favor the solidification and expansion of the Order, an adaptation that the papacy considered necessary and valid. In 1230, with an official papal declaration, the Bull *Quo elongati*, Gregory IX decreed that Francis' *Testament* had no binding force as a juridical document. The friars were required to observe only those counsels of the Gospel included as precepts of the *Rule*.

By this Bull, the Pope also approved the office of a money-manager for the friars since the *Rule* forbad the friars' accepting money.[16] This *nuntius* was a layperson who acted as an agent of the friars' benefactors in disposing of money-alms, using the money to provide for the friars' needs without obliging the friars to handle the money themselves. The permission to use the offices of the *nuntius* kept the friars legally poor (the funds were in the hands of a person outside the Order) while allowing what amounted to

---

16   *Ibid.*, p. 58.

fund-raising programs for building projects and for housing and feeding large numbers, particularly in the large study centers. In practice, friars began more and more to achieve a security which to some seemed clearly a violation of the spirit, if not the letter, of the *Rule*.

The Bull also used a distinction between "ownership" and "use" to soothe the consciences of the friars while favoring the Order's growth and financial stability. According to *Quo elongati*, the friars had the use of things (buildings, books, churches, etc.) while the legal ownership of these things remained in the hands of others, the donors themselves, or the Church.[17] In practice, however, the friars gradually became the real owners of property as the issue of ownership became a legal fiction. This development deeply disturbed those like the Spirituals who saw in radical non-ownership the core of the Franciscan vow of poverty.

Reformers demanded a return to the "literal" observance of the *Rule*, eliminating the office of the financial intermediaries. They looked with distrust on the expansion of studies and the growing "parochial" ministry in the city churches. They offered a greater sphere of activity to the lay friars, some of whom were leaders in the reform movement. Calling for a return to the contemplative character of the Franciscan life, they had a special love for the hermitages, in which some of their most revered members lived.

In choosing to emphasize these parts of the Franciscan life, they drew inspiration not only from the Rule but also from the *Testament* of Francis. In this document, written shortly before his death, Francis recalled his own conversion and the brothers' early form of life. He emphasized the continuing duty of the friars to live according to that pattern he had chosen, especially in the

---

17   *Ibid.*, pp. 56-60.

practice of poverty. After his death papal decrees like *Quo elongati* solicited by the Order clarified that this *Testament* was not legally binding on the friars. It was to be considered an exhortation and not a sanctioned juridical statement of the founder about the life of the Order.

The reformers, nevertheless, appealed to the testimony of this exhortation as evidently revealing the mind of Francis. Therefore, though it might not be legally binding, it was certainly morally binding on those who wished to observe the *Rule* "spiritually." (The reformers' insistence on this "spiritual" observance earned them their name, Spirituals.) They also justified their position by appealing to the *Rule* itself, especially the famous Chapter Ten on obedience. Here they reasoned that the ministers, by accepting papal concessions regarding fund raising and ignoring Francis' *Testament*, were now effectively obliging the friars to live in a way contrary to their consciences and the *Rule* itself. These were precisely the conditions under which, Francis wrote, the friars were no longer bound to obey the ministers. Finding that they "could not observe the *Rule* spiritually" where they were, they had "recourse to the ministers" who did not, however, "receive them kindly." Their dilemma was that already mentioned: should they obey the ministers or the *Rule*?

They chose the latter, and their disobedience soon set in motion a machinery of persecution and oppression, juridical, moral, and even physical.

In 1274 a rumor spread that the Pope, Gregory X, at the Council of Lyon, would annul the provisions that the mendicant Orders could not own property. The rumor alarmed some friars in the province of the Marches, the mountainous area near Ancona in northeastern Italy. The rumored annulment was not carried out in regard to the Franciscans, yet it raised a serious question. Did the Pope have the authority to do such a thing?[18]

Some friars reasoned in this way: if the poverty chosen by Francis, radically that of non-ownership, is the same poverty as that of Christ and the apostles, can the Pope dispense the friars from observing it? "No" was their conclusion: the Pope can no more change the *Rule* than the Gospel.

This attitude may appear odd to today's reader—there would seem to be a notable difference between the *Rule* of the Franciscans and the Gospel of Jesus Christ. The difference was not, however, so apparent in the thirteenth century. To understand the differences between that mentality and ours, an excursus is in order to help us appreciate how intimately the issue of the *Rule* was identified with the question of salvation itself.

The Drama of the Rule

In the "quest for salvation" of the thirteenth century, Francis and his brothers inherited the spiritual patrimony of the twelfth century. During that time reformers sought those sure norms which would guarantee that their way of life was that practiced by and transmitted from the earliest Christians.[19]

The search for the "apostolic life" focussed attention on the life of the apostles after Pentecost, the life of the primitive Christian community. This had also been the model for Christian monasticism but, at least in the West, there were new interpretations of the "apostolic life" that did not fit within the

---

18   See Giacinto Pagnani, *San Liberato e il suo convento (con ampi cenni sui rapporti tra i comuni di S. Ginesio e Sarnano e il movimento degli spirituali nelle Marche)* (Falconara: Edizioni Biblioteca Francescana, 1962), p. 16.

19   See the very interesting study of this search in Henrietta Leyser's *The Lay Hermit Movements of the 11th and 12th Centuries* (Oxford: 1981).

ordinary structures of prevailing Benedictine monastic life. Among the newly emphasized elements were those of poverty especially and of public preaching.

If the *Rule of Benedict*, the prime religious *Rule* of the West, did not provide these elements sufficiently, where could one find the "rule of life" that most fully incorporated all the essential elements? One reformer after another responded, "The Gospel is the rule of life." The Canons Regular in their various branches followed this course, eventually adopting the *Rule of St. Augustine* for their organizational model. Likewise the Grandmontines and similar movements incorporated elements from earlier monastic tradition with the renewed emphasis on poverty and preaching in their form of "apostolic life."

An early Franciscan text called the "Assisi Compilation" (Chapter 18) sketched a dramatic moment in the history of the new *Rule of the Lesser Brothers* which Francis presented to the Pope for approval. Advised to choose from among the religious *Rules* already existing (the Fourth Lateran Council had forbidden new ones), Francis replied: "Do not talk to me about Bernard or Augustine or Benedict because the Lord has chosen me to be a new kind of fool in this world." In writing his *Rule*, Francis would show his commitment to embracing the Gospel itself as the structure for the life of his new Order. The text begins with these words: "The Rule and Life of the Friars Minor is this, namely to observe the Holy Gospel of Our Lord Jesus Christ…"[20]

The original "form of life" proposed by Francis in 1209 and approved verbally by Innocent III does not exist. It was apparently a simple collection of texts from the Gospels. The Rule drawn up in 1221 has long sections of the Gospels and other Scriptural

---

20   Armstrong-Brady, p. 137.

quotations spun through it. The officially approved *Rule* of 1223, while showing the hand of a juridical advisor (probably Cardinal Ugolino, later Pope Gregory IX) still shows that basically the Gospel and its demands remain the norm of living for the brothers.

Characteristic of this *Rule* was its emphatic conviction of the necessity of absolute poverty in order to live the Gospel. It represented a shift of focus from the model of the early Church to the model of Jesus himself. Whereas the Church of Jerusalem as described in Acts was one in which "they held all things in common," the "Church" of Jesus, Mary and the apostles described in the Gospels was one in which the members had nothing, neither staff nor purse, nor an extra tunic. The Master himself had "no place to lay his head," and the band travelled from place to place, shaking the dust from their feet if they were not given hospitality.

Against the protestations of some who claimed that such a way of life was "impossible," its supporters could counter that to make such a claim was to deny the possibility of anyone's living the Gospel.

Francis' followers gradually developed a theory of their *Rule* in which it was extolled as the most perfect synthesis of the Gospel. In fact, they claimed, it was superior to existing *Rules* because it led to a life according to the example of Christ himself. Its model was, therefore, pre-ecclesial or proto-ecclesial, the life of the "historical Jesus" and his companions, Mary and the Twelve, during the years before the birth of the Church at Pentecost.

The Franciscan *Rule* was, therefore, a very sure "guide to salvation." Following its prescriptions would lead one to conformity with the life of Christ himself, particularly in the practice of the same poverty practiced by the Lord, his mother and the apostles.

The Crisis of 1274

This excursus on the *Rule's* identification of the Franciscan life with the life of Christ and his early followers helps to clarify the intensity with which the *Rule* was promoted and extolled. With the rumors in 1274 of a papal declaration granting exemption from the *Rule's* proscription of property ownership, some friars were quick to see such an action as dispensing from the witness of poverty in the Gospel. That would effectively set aside the example of Christ as normative for salvation. Here was one of the points of conflict which would soon pit sectors of the friars against other groups within the Order and even against the papacy they had vowed to respect and obey in the same *Rule*.

The problem was particularly acute in the Province of the Marches. The heated remarks of a few friars about the Pope's rights in this matter sounded suspiciously close to that religious treason called heresy in the Middle Ages.

Threatened with severe punishments by their ministers, most retracted their statements. Three who refused were stripped of the habit and imprisoned in remote hermitages for a year. At the end of their sentence they reported to the superiors with an ambiguous declaration of fidelity sufficient to guarantee their safety after a three-day trial. They soon resumed their criticisms, however, and were arrested again. Their movement was spreading, creating a serious problem in the relations between the Order and the Holy See. A court of ministers was assembled to resolve the issue and found the outspoken friars guilty, imposing on them a drastic sentence: the leaders were condemned to life imprisonment and excommunicated. They were deprived of all books including those for the recitation of the Divine Office; at their deaths they were to be denied Christian burial. The brothers assigned to guard them were forbidden to speak to them and were to check the locks on their cells twice a day to prevent escape attempts. The sentence against them was to be read weekly to all the friars in their local chapters and any who dared to criticize its provisions were to suffer the same punishment as the rebels.[21]

The condemned friars were Pietro (sometimes called Liberato) da Macerata, Tommaso da Tolentino, "a certain Brother Trasmondo," and a later follower of the movement, Pietro da Fossombrone. This last-mentioned friar is better known to history by the name he adopted later, Angelo Clareno. For the next fifty years of his life (he died in 1337) Angelo experienced the full consequences of his obstinate attachment to the "literal observance" of the *Rule*. He came to be known as the "father of the Spirituals."[22]

The severity of the measures soon claimed another victim. Brother Tommaso da Castel d'Emilio protested at the reading of the sentence: "This is iniquitous and unjust, contrary to the law of God and offensive to the saints." On hearing his protest, those present rose immediately, stripped off his habit, and locked him in a windowless cell. Maltreated and sick, he soon died. Faithful to the sentence inflicted on malcontents, the friars unceremoniously threw his body into a ditch, "covering it with dirt so that secular persons would not see it."[23]

After more than ten years of imprisonment the rebel leaders were freed through the intervention of a Minister General sympathetic to their cause. Sent as missionaries to Armenia,

21 Pagnani, p. 18.

22 *Ibid.*

23 Alberto Ghinato, *La Cronaca d'Angelo Clareno* (Rome: 1959) pp. 151-55, cited in Pagnani, p. 19.

they were persecuted there also by their brethren. Two of them returned to their province of the Marches where they were shunned by all.[24]

Their salvation came from an unexpected direction, the papacy itself, in the person of the newly-elected Pope Celestine V. Having lived as a hermit himself, he approved of their plans and wished to protect them from persecution. He officially separated them from the Franciscan superiors and made them an independent body, The Hermits of Pope Celestine or, as they were known later, Friars of the Poor Life of Celestine V. People also called them "little friars," *fraticelli*, a name that would soon become synonymous with heresy and treason against the Church. Unfortunately for them, Celestine resigned after five months. With his "poor hermits" the former Pope set out for Apulia in the South of Italy with the hope of reaching Greece. The new Pope, Boniface VIII, had other plans: his troops took Celestine to the isolated sanctuary of Mount Gargano where a group of angry friars berated him for sanctioning the first division of the Franciscan Order.[25]

The "poor hermits" did make their way to Greece. Fleeing their former confreres along the coast, they moved to Thessaly where, among the Orthodox, they found some peace. Angelo Clareno there dedicated himself to the study of Greek and the forms of Orthodox monastic life.

Later Developments

The typical mark of the Spirituals was the short, shabby habit, their insistence on the "poor use" (*usus pauper*) of goods, and

---

24   Pagnani, p. 20.

25   *Ibid.*, pp. 22-23.

observance of the Rule literally, without glosses or interpretations. The habit became their symbol, "patched within and without with sacking" according to Francis' recommendation in the *Rule*, and based on the practice of the early companions. Regarding the *usus pauper* they insisted that, besides non-ownership, a somewhat facile juridical statement of fact, poverty demanded the intrinsically poor value of things used by the friars.

Ubertino da Casale served as the theoretician who drew from these rich materials the principles of Franciscan life. In 1310, in the Introduction to his work, *Sanctitas vestra*, he enumerates the seven fundamental qualities on which the Order rests:

> ...in highest and hence pacific poverty; in most innocent simplicity, and thereby it eschews all subtlety and cunning; in spotless purity, hence set apart from the din of the world; in deep humility, whereby it avoids superiority, and anything inimical to respect for the hierarchy; in assiduous prayer and work, defence against distraction, idleness, greed and worldliness; in perfect charity, defence against mutual persecution and hatred; in being an example to others, and hence avoiding offence to the faint-hearted among the laity.[26]

The friars of the Spiritual party heard in these words an authentic call to return to fundamentals, to recover a vision and virtues that no longer characterized the Order of the early fourteenth century. But besides these seven qualities of the Order, the Spirituals also insisted on a number of other issues. Ubertino pushed to their limits the teachings of the brilliant polemicist

---

26   The full text in *Archiv fur Literatur und Kirchengeschichte des Mittelalters*, ed. H. Denifle, F. Ehrle, 7 vols. (Berlin/Freiburg-i-B., 1885-1900), III, 51-89, quoted in Nimmo 95-6.

from Provence, Friar Peter John Olivi. Ubertino identified the "poor use" with the teaching of the Gospel itself, suggesting that those opposed to it might even be considered heretics. Exiled at La Verna because of his dangerous views, in seven months he composed his major work, the *Tree of Life (Arbor vitae crucifixae Iesu)*. The book contains remarkable pages on Jesus worthy of the greatest mystics, alongside apocalyptic fulminations against Church and popes, and visions of the Sixth Age of the World with the return of St. Francis and his combat against the Antichrist.[27]

Following the lead of such authors as Ubertino, the Spirituals intended to observe the *Rule* literally without the "glosses," papal declarations which favored adaptation, expansion and parochialization of the Order. Their attitude was based, as we might expect, on fidelity to their beloved moral charter, Francis' *Testament*. The problem of ecclesiastical authority was here inevitably raised, since the glosses were issued by the Pope himself, and not infrequently the Spirituals tended to see papal declarations as the cause of the Order's collapse in discipline. Besides, the papal declarations were not being observed anyway.

The Spirituals suffered more and more severe persecution from the friars of the Community between 1270 and 1289. For a few years, between 1289 and 1295, they had a sympathizer in Minister General Raymond Godefroy of Provence. After his term of office they were persecuted again until a partial truce was reached under Clement V between 1309 and 1312, as he attempted to impose on the whole Order a compromise based on a "moderate observance" of the *Rule*. In 1313 a group of Tuscan Spirituals, impatient with the pace of reform, revolted and took over three houses of their Province as their own. Fearing the reaction of the

---

27   Vorreux p. 291.

Order and the papacy, some fled soon afterward to Sicily.

In April of the same year Pope Clement asked the Chapter to elect a Minister General who would be favorable toward the Spirituals and received an answer in the person of Alessandro of Alessandria. He gave the reformers three houses in Provence, those of Narbonne, Béziers and Carcassone, allowing them some protection from the persecution of their brethren. In 1314 both the Pope and the General died and during the succeeding two years' vacancy of both offices, the Spirituals suffered again at the hands of the friars of the Community, losing the few houses that had been given to them. Soon they revolted also in Provence, as their fellows had done in Tuscany, retaking the houses of Narbonne and Béziers and driving out their opponents. The rebels were accused of being schismatics, apostates and heretics and were placed under interdict and excommunicated.

In 1316 a new Pope and a new Minister General took office: John XXII and Michael of Cesena. They decided upon a complete suppression of the Spirituals. In 1317, with the Bull *Sancta romana*, Angelo Clareno's congregation was officially suppressed (though they remained active). Those known as *fraticelli* were excommunicated (including both dissident Spirituals such as those of Angelo's group and the *beguines* or *bizzocchi*, their lay supporters). The Tuscan friar fugitives in Sicily were ordered arrested; the Spirituals of Provence were declared guilty of heresy and condemned. On May 7, 1318, the last four of these Spirituals holding out against the Inquisition were burned alive in the market square of Marseilles.[28]

In 1322 Pope John declared that the Order was in fact the owner of some of the property it used, effectively declaring

---

28   Nimmo, p. 174.

that it contradicted the *Rule* it professed. In 1323 the same Pope issued the Bull *Cum inter nonnullos* denying the absolute poverty of Christ and the apostles. At this point, the Pope had gone too far in the opinion even of some who had opposed the Spirituals. Michael of Cesena, the Minister General; Bonagratia of Bergamo, an outstanding spokesman of the Community party; and the English scholar William of Ockham united in their condemnation of the Pope.

During the next fifty years the Order endured a period of steady decline. The period following the break with John XXII can be considered one of both ferment and dissolution. Scandalous laxity and abuse appeared in sectors of the Community while the undercurrent of the dissident *fraticelli* remained, and two diverse groups began to cooperate: the older Spirituals and the newer followers of Michael of Cesena and William of Ockham after their break with John XXII in 1328.

Many of them moved to the edges of the Church: to Armenia, Syria, Persia and Greece. Angelo Clareno himself returned to Italy and was befriended by the Benedictine Abbot of Subiaco and after 1317 made his home in a hermitage near the *Sacro Speco* there—dedicating himself to directing his far-flung followers and writing his version of the events that had led to his exile in his *History of the Seven Tribulations of the Order of Friars Minor.* His followers continued to wear the short ragged habit which had already become their symbol and lived in remote hermitages, often under the protection of local authorities, both ecclesiastical and civil. Under pressure from the Inquisitors, Angelo eventually left Subiaco to die in the Kingdom of Naples in 1337.

The Observants and the
Revival of Early Ideals

In the 1330s another movement for reform began to grow, with its center in the area south of Assisi, the region of Foligno, bordering the area that provided a home to Angelo Clareno and his disciples. The movement was that of the Observance, meaning a "stricter observance" of the Franciscan *Rule*. The leader responsible for its acceptance and growth was Paolo dei Trinci, known by his nickname, "Paoluccio,""little Paul."

Paoluccio was born in 1309 to the family of the Trinci, lords of Foligno. One of his uncles was bishop of Foligno, another was the bishop of neighboring Spoleto. In 1323 Paoluccio joined the Order at Foligno, at the age of fourteen. Shortly after Paoluccio, a man named John of Valle joined the Order also at Foligno. In that community we know there was also a friar Gentile of Spoleto. These three men in different ways would affect the future of the Observant reform.[29]

Paoluccio, the son of nobility, chose the life of a lay friar; this meant a life of menial chores, domestic work in the friary and church, prayer, poverty and begging. Like Paoluccio, Gentile was a lay friar. John of Valle was ordained to the priesthood after joining the Order. These three held in common a certain ideal of "reformed life." This desire for reform was shared and encouraged by others, for example, another lay friar of the local community, Blessed Tommaso of Foligno and, as counsellor and friend from a distance, Angelo Clareno.[30]

In 1334 the Minister General, Geraldus Odonis, gave his permission for John and Gentile to retire to a remote hermitage

---

29   *Ibid.*, pp. 364-368.

30   *Ibid.*, pp. 368-370.

at Brogliano, in the rugged hill country northeast of Foligno. There John lived peacefully, perhaps with a few companions, in an austere, contemplative life for nearly twenty years, until his death in 1351.

By 1346 the General Chapter at Venice was ready to express cautious support for the movement which had spread to a few other hermitages in the twelve years since John and Gentile had retired to Brogliano. Perhaps it was during this period of growth that Paoluccio dei Trinci joined the movement, either at Brogliano itself or at one of the affiliated hermitages.[31]

The support of the Order for the reform was, however, short-lived. By 1350 encouragement had changed to suspicion. Apparently the Community resumed its former attitude of distrust or at least threatened to break up the homogeneity of the membership in the reform communities. For whatever reason, Gentile of Spoleto, now superior of the hermitage of the Carceri, invoked papal protection to safeguard members of the nascent reform. Clement VI responded by granting autonomy to Gentile against "the interference of the Order's superiors."[32]

This papal intervention alarmed the friars of the Community. At the recommendation of the 1354 Assisi General Chapter, the newly-elected Minister General, William Farinier, started to investigate the group. They had adopted the distinctive short habit associated with the Spirituals, they refused him obedience, and they harbored heretics (avowedly to reform them). Accordingly the General procured a reversal of the papal decision to protect them. He ordered the reform disbanded; its members were to return to the "ordinary" communities of the Province. Gentile was

---

31   *Ibid.*, p. 387.

32   *Ibid.*, p. 386.

arrested at Orvieto and imprisoned there until shortly before his death in 1362 (at Brogliano, his old home). At this time Paoluccio returned to the Foligno friary where he had lived previously.[33]

Returning to Foligno, Paoluccio was mistreated by his confreres. According to one story his uncle, Lord Ugolino, saw him black and blue from a beating and put him in a tower in his garden for rest and recuperation. His superiors eventually gave their permission for him to remain there. His holiness, penitential life and perseverance earned him respect, not only among the citizens of Foligno but also among an increasing number of the friars there.

A ruse, not the only one in Franciscan history, allowed Paoluccio to pursue his ideal. His cousin, Lord of Foligno, had insisted on hosting the Chapter for the friars of Umbria at Foligno, at his own expense. Having already provided most generously for the friars during the whole time of the Chapter, he hosted the Minister General, a personal friend, at a final reception at the conclusion of the Chapter's sessions. Grateful for his host's generosity, the Minister expressed the thanks of the whole Order to Lord Trinci and assured him that if he should ever have a request to make of the Order it would surely be granted. The nobleman had waited patiently for this moment and immediately made a simple request: that his cousin, Paoluccio, be allowed to take up residence at the dilapidated hermitage of Brogliano in a desolate area on the border of the Trinci family estates. The Minister readily granted what appeared to be a quite modest

---

33   We may note that during this storm the name of John of Valle and the hermitage of Brogliano were not mentioned. Presumably someone was still living there in 1362, when Gentile was released from prison and was allowed to stay there until his death shortly afterward. By 1368 it seems to have been empty once again. See Nimmo, p. 393.

favor to such a liberal benefactor.

That very evening, however, when the community of the local friary heard of his acquiescence to the lord's request, they alarmed the Minister by pointing to the lethal danger of a "secessionist movement" if Paoluccio were allowed to realize his plan for a "stricter observance" of the *Rule*. The Minister dutifully returned to the lord the next day, asking him to make some other request and not to hold to the agreement made the previous day. At this point, however, Lord Trinci showed a very different and determined attitude. He would hold the Minister General of the Order, his friend, to his word.

The Minister had already lost face by attempting to deny a favor he had already freely granted. Now he also risked losing the benevolence of a powerful friend and influential benefactor. He could only reconfirm with embarrassment the favor he had just tried to refuse. (The components of the little drama—a powerful noble, a hermitage, an unwilling Minister—will figure again in the subsequent history of reforms in the Franciscan Family in the story of the "Friars of the Eremitical Life," the Capuchins).

Paoluccio retired to Brogliano and quietly revived the Observant reform initiated by John of Valle and nearly destroyed by Gentile of Spoleto.

"With four or five companions," he set up residence at Brogliano. Within a short time all the others decided to leave the experiment and he remained alone for some time. His life there was one of prayer and poverty, a reformed life with the permission of his superiors. Gradually heartier new recruits arrived and, from 1370 to 1380, the movement grew quickly. By 1373 eleven hermitages were allied to Paoluccio's community of Brogliano. The new Pope Gregory XI looked favorably on the reform, particularly as a fully orthodox alternative to the heterodox *fraticelli*.

By 1374 both the Pope and the new Minister General, Leonardo of Giffoni, favored the reform movement. In 1380, Paoluccio was empowered by the Provincial and the General to control the reformed group and to extend it throughout the country. Paoluccio and his followers, among whom a notable number were lay friars, were called "the simple brothers," *fratres simplices*. Their life revealed the characteristic elements of Franciscan renewal movements: the importance of hermitages, the presence of lay friars, a desire for a genuinely poor life. The attractiveness of their reforming ideal, blessed with the approval of Pope and Minister General, led to rapidly increasing numbers. By the time of Paoluccio's death in 1391, the Observant movement was an important feature in the geography of the Franciscan world.

Beneath the tides of Franciscan reforming activity, another current was noticeable toward the end of the fourteenth century. The tradition of Franciscan spiritual writing began to expand its influence, making a mark on the devotional life of the faithful. The figure of Francis was presented as a model worthy of imitation, a guide (like his *Rule*) to union with Christ. The notion of Francis as "another Christ" (*alter Christus*) glorified the memory of the saint of Assisi and served to elevate the prestige of the Order he founded. An important book of the time stated the case eloquently. Written between 1385 and 1390 by a friar, Bartholomew of Pisa, the work was called *The Book of the Conformities of the Blessed Francis with the Life of the Lord Jesus*. In the *Conformities* its well-educated author used biographical sources for the life of Francis to show the ways in which the saint's life reproduced events of the life of Christ. The *Conformities* was a popular success in its day, but two centuries later it became a target for the Reformation's criticisms of the cult of the saints. Voltaire and the Encyclopedists in the eighteenth century would also attack Bartholomew's work citing it as a typical example of religious sectarianism and obscurantism.[34]

Despite such attacks, the arms of the Order still carry the "Conformities," the crossed arms on a bare cross, symbolizing Christ and Francis. This appreciation of the conformity of Francis to the Crucified Christ fueled the imagination of generations of Franciscan artists and writers who followed the example set by Bartholomew's work.

Observants and Conventuals

Our next glimpse at the complex story of the "Franciscan Dialectic" shows us the Observants in the century after Paoluccio's death. Bernardine of Siena, a great popular preacher and tireless promoter of the Observants, was received into the Order in 1402, and by his death he had founded three hundred friaries containing some four thousand Observant friars. Ten years after his death in 1444, the Observants numbered some twenty thousand. Though some have characterized the Observant movement as "a true reform, a rejuvenation, not a rupture,"[35] in the century following the modest beginning at Brogliano, Paoluccio's success was leading to another deep division in the Order, that between Observants and Conventuals.

The latter name referred to those friars who resided in the urban "convents" and study centers of the Order and who were heavily committed to parochial ministry and to University life. They allowed use of concessions from the popes, notably those

---

34 Erasmus Alber, also known as Alberus. wrote a polemical work called "The Franciscans' Koran," with a preface by Luther, including stinging attacks on the *Conformities*. See Vorreux, p. 292.

35 Vorreux, p. 298.

granted in the Apostolic Brief *Ad Statum* of August 23, 1430, which gave friars the right to possess property and receive fixed revenues. These were concessions that Observants pointedly refused to use. As the differences between the two parties increased, the first signs of separation between the two branches of the Order appeared. In 1443, just a year before Bernardine of Siena died, the Observants gained the right to be governed by their own Vicar General. This arrangement practically removed them from the authority of the Minister General of the Order, chosen from among the Conventual friars.

Their gaining of near-autonomy served to confirm that the Observant reform had now become an institution in its own right, a powerful and influential body, practically independent from the friars of what was called the Conventual body of the Order. As the prestige and numbers of the Observants increased, their desire for full independence grew.

In 1517 the reigning Pope, Leo X, convoked the General Chapter of the Order at the friary of Ara Coeli in Rome.[36] Leo intended to promote uniformity *and* reform by favoring the members of the Observant Movement. His goal was to be reached in two steps: uniting all reform movements under the leadership of the Observants, and declaring that this amalgamation of reformed friars now formed the "officially recognized" Order.[37]

Perhaps he hoped that friars who did not belong to one of the reform movements would nevertheless conform themselves to the new arrangement and would ally themselves with the reformers. There would be a change in the leadership—but the Order would

36 For those familiar with the city of Rome, this friary is attached to the church above Piazza Venezia, obscured by the Victor Emmanuel Monument built on its former grounds.

37 Iriarte, p. 74.

remain under one Minister General.

Perhaps this was his hope. If so, he was disappointed. The Chapter instead became a battle between two major groups. The first was that of the "conventual communities," that is, friars who followed the *Rule* and accepted, legitimately, those official papal pronouncements which allowed exception to the *Rule's* proscription of commonly held property. The second major group was that headed by the "Observants," who followed the same *Rule* but chose, also legitimately, not to make use of the exceptions granted by papal documents.

The issue, at least at first glance, was that of poverty. But a deeper issue was that of reform itself. (We must keep in mind that in that same year Luther proposed his reforms in Wittenberg.)

The Chapter's results marked another step in the "scandal" of Franciscan history. With the Bull *Ite vos* delivered to the 1517 Chapter, Leo recognized canonically a separation already existing in fact. The Order was divided into the Order of Friars Minor, and the Order of Minors Conventual. The latter were to have a Master General (like that of the Dominicans) subject to the confirmation of the Minister General of the reorganized Order of Friars Minor, that of Observants and allied reformers. The move was clearly an insult to the former, and was hailed as a triumph by the latter.

However we judge the wisdom or necessity of Leo's decision, we must still recognize in the events of 1517 a sad day in the history of the Franciscan Family, and one whose effects would sanction division after division among the friars and among the Poor Sisters and Penitents allied with them.

The Conventual friars, after this humiliating decision, soon restored the title of Minister General and were freed from any dependence on the Observants. There were now, in practice, two Orders of Friars Minor with two Ministers General and two sets of legislation: two Orders following the same *Rule* under the inspiration of the same founder, living and working in the same territory, each intent on destroying the credibility and effectiveness of the other.

Leo had called for uniformity besides reform and directed that the newly-united reform groups, organized under the umbrella of the Observance, should publish legislation to be observed by all. But here yet another division appeared: the friars "beyond the Alps" (Ultramontanes) led by the Spanish and French, and friars "below the Alps" (Cismontanes), led by the Italians, could not agree on uniform legislation. The differences were markedly national in character. Spanish friars dominated the Ultramontanes as their nation bid for European supremacy. The friars of France tried, unsuccessfully, to break the control of the Spanish over the Order's life in Europe "beyond the Alps."[38]

The Order sanctioned national divisions by legislating that the Minister General, elected every six years, must be chosen alternately from the Ultramontane and Cismontane friars. Further, when the General was an Ultramontane, the Cismontane friars would be governed by their own General Commissary. A parallel arrangement would prevail when a Cismontane was General. In practice this meant an Italian General with a Spanish Vicar General to be succeeded by a Spanish General with an Italian Vicar.[39]

The two geographical "families," besides relative autonomy of government, also developed different legislation. The Cismontanes issued twelve different sets of General Constitutions

---

38 *Ibid.*, pp. 170-171.

39 *Ibid*, p. 170.

by 1700, the Ultramontanes, three. Provinces began to issue their own "Statutes" and, while seeking by this means to insure stability, only exacerbated the difficulties of establishing common legislation in the Order.

The Observants grew in the seventeenth century so that the number of friars of the Regular Observance (the main branch) reached 34,900; various smaller sub-groups allied with the movement (to be discussed below) made up another 28,500. All members of the Observance thus numbered 63,400 as they entered the eighteenth century.

The Retiros

Other questions of reform were simmering beneath the surface during the dramatic events of 1517. What Lázaro Iriarte has called "the perennial lure of the eremitical life," always renewed and always overcome in Franciscan reforms, was an issue about to provoke new divisions in the Order "unified" by Leo's decisions.[40]

The background to this story takes us from Italy to Spain. A Spanish friar named Juan de la Puebla (d. 1495) had lived at the hermitage of the Carceri near Assisi for several years. On returning to Spain, he founded *retiros* or houses of retreat in the *Extremadura*, land of conquistadors and adventurers, and a hotbed of fervent reformers.[41]

In 1487 Juan received papal permission to found a custody (a semi-autonomous body within a province) dedicated to Our Lady of the Angels. As the *retiros* multiplied quickly, Observant leaders grew suspicious and tried to ensure that the flourishing contemplative communities remained within the structures of

---

40   *Ibid.*, p. 172.

41   *Ibid.*

the Observance.

Juan de Guadalupe (d. 1506) a disciple in this *retiro* movement, grew dissatisfied with the authority of the Observants' leadership. He wished to move beyond their "regular Observance" to the "strictest Observance," thereby indicating that the Observant reform had already become an institution needing reform itself. In 1496 he received papal permission to retire with some companions to hermitages near Granada in order to "observe the Gospel and the *Rule* in complete poverty, wearing the same habit as St. Francis," under the authority of the Minister General alone (that is, without depending on the Observant leadership).[42]

Members of this reform insisted on wearing the same kind of habit as Francis and the earliest friars, a question that earlier fired the imagination of the Spirituals. For Juan, this consisted in a shorter tunic than was then in use with a cone-shaped hood and a short cape, all of which were mended inside and out with materials of various colors. Furthermore they insisted that the friars go barefoot disallowing even sandals. From this practice, they earned their name of "shoeless" (discalced) friars. They were also called "Guadalupe friars" (*Guadalupenses*), especially in Spain, and "hoods"(*Capuchos*) in Portugal.[43]

In the years following their foundation the Discalced Friars experienced several organizational problems. The Observants obtained a papal ruling that this new reform must remain under their former superiors of the Observance (1502); the Discalced had the decision overturned (1506). They gained the right to form an independent Custody under friars of the Conventual branch (1506), and the Observants obtained a new papal ruling

---

42   *Ibid.*, p. 175.

43   *Ibid.*

demanding the reformers either return to the Observance or leave Spain and Portugal (also 1506). The Discalced won another victory by obtaining permission to form an independent Province (1508).[44]

With his "Bull of Union," Leo X incorporated the Discalced friars into the Observance in 1517 while allowing them to have two provinces of their own, one in Spain (*Extremadura*) and the other in Portugal. Not all the Discalced were pleased with this solution. One of their members, Juan Pascual, in that same turbulent year of reorganization asked permission of the newly-designated Master General of the Conventuals to start a group of Reformed Conventual Friars. The movement was approved and began to grow, receiving special papal permission to accept into their reform Observant friars and members of other Orders "of mitigated observance."[45]

The greatest fame of the Spanish Discalced Reform came to it through Peter of Alcantara (d. 1562). Having served his term as Minister Provincial in the Observant family, Peter planned to retire to a solitary, contemplative life of penitence. When his Observant superiors opposed this plan, Peter received papal permission to transfer to the Conventual friars whose General named him General Commissary of the Reformed Conventuals. Founding a hermitage with its own statutes, Peter shaped the houses of this reform movement into a Custody and later a Province (San José) in 1559, under the Conventual General. In 1563, after Peter's death, these reformed friars were placed under the Observant General, though keeping their own statutes and habit. They were called both by the generic name, Discalced Friars, and after Peter's death,

---

44   *Ibid.*, p. 176.

45   *Ibid.*

Alcantarines.[46]

As their movement grew through Spain and Portugal to Italy, the Americas and Asia (they had responsibility for the Philippine mission), the Discalced friars gained greater autonomy of government but never became a separate Order. Governed by their own Constitutions rather than the General Constitutions, they were subject only to the Minister General of the Observants, each province maintaining one representative in their common residence at the friary of St. Isidore in Rome. In 1700 the Discalced numbered six thousand five-hundred members.[47]

The Reformed

In 1502, the Observant Vicar General, Martial Boulier, decreed that all the provinces of Spain must have houses of recollection, and these became subsequently more or less numerous throughout the country. The *retiro* movement spread to Italy beginning in 1518 with the encouragement of the General, Francesco Lichetto. However, it encountered opposition after his death from his successor, Paolo da Soncino.

One of Juan de la Puebla's disciples, Francisco Quiñones, elected Minister General in 1523, tried to promote this movement in the Order at large. Had he continued in this task the movement might have remained within the Order. He arrived in Italy in 1525, and offered his protection to the houses of recollection giving them statutes similar to those of the Spanish *retiros*.[48]

His Italian successor, Paolo Pisotti, was completely opposed to the movement. Disliked for his violent and arbitrary form of

---

46   *Ibid.*, p. 177.

47   *Ibid.*, p. 229.

48   *Ibid.*, p. 173.

government, he was deposed by Clement VII before completing his term of office.

The opposition of the Italian superiors to the *retiro* movement over more than fifteen years led to the establishment of two reform groups seeking greater autonomy: the "Friars of the Eremitical Life" (Capuchins) and the "Reformed Friars Minor" (*Riformati*). Many of the leading friars of the houses of recollection in Italy joined these two groups.

After deposing Pisotti, Clement VII moved to protect the struggling houses of recollection. He ruled that every province must have houses in which friars could observe a very strict interpretation of the *Rule*, could wear rough and patched habits, and go barefoot. The friars belonging to these reformed custodies were known simply as Reformed friars (*Riformati*). Their houses were united into a custody within each province, and their superior, or Custos, represented them at the Provincial Chapter.[49]

Despite these favorable regulations, the *Riformati* did not flourish at first except in Northern Italy. Spreading their message north from that base, they gradually gained adherents in Germany and Austria.

The opposition of Italian superiors changed to support in 1535, when the General Chapter voted its confidence to the houses of recollection. This change of attitude favored their expansion and also kept within the Order and its provinces those friars attracted to what was, after all, an exemplary form of life.

As the members of the *Riformati* increased during the next fifty years, so did their desire for greater independence. Like the Discalced in Spain, the Reformed in Italy were released in 1579 from the authority of the Observant superiors on the provincial

49   *Ibid.*, p. 174

level and depended solely on the Minister General. Their superiors could accept any Observant friars without consulting the Observant Provincial and could demand houses from the Provincial. Once "reformed," a friar could not return to the Observants. These wide powers granted to the Reformed alarmed the superiors of the Observants.[50]

The Minister General, Francesco Gonzaga, obtained the revocation of the papal ruling within a year. He then advised the Observant Provincials to treat the Reformed with kindness, and over the next decade worked diligently to remove the causes of discontent within the Observant system while publishing special statutes for the Reformed in 1582.

With the intervention of Clement VIII in 1596, the Reformed finally gained complete independence from the Observant Provincials. They were now to be governed by their own superiors, while still recognizing the authority of the Observant Minister General.

The Minister General at the time, Bonaventura da Caltagirone, attempted unsuccessfully to prevent this new division of the Order, first making a juridical protest, then offering such concessions as the establishment of autonomous Reformed Provinces, and finally encouraging a "pamphlet war" against the Reformed friars. Even the General Chapter of 1600 attempted to reach a mutually agreeable solution, but without success.[51]

The Reformed soon received papal approval for their own Vicar General and General Chapter. Their allegiance to the authority of the Observant Minister General had by now become merely nominal. Once having gained this organizational autonomy,

---

50   *Ibid.*, pp. 178-179.

51   *Ibid.*, p. 179.

the Reformed friars spread their movement rapidly. In Central Europe their growth was notable: in 1623 two custodies formed in Poland parallel to the Observant Provinces. Entire provinces switched allegiance from the Observance to the Reform: Bavaria in 1625, Tyrol in 1628, Austria in 1632, Bohemia in 1660, Croatia in 1688. A compromise in government was reached in 1639: while the Observant Minister General was acknowledged as holding full authority over the Reformed, he must govern them according to special statutes and must always choose the Vicar General of the Order from among the Reformed.[52]

The Recollects

The movement toward houses of recollection flourished in Spain under the banner of the Discalced and in Italy and Central Europe under the name of the Reformed. In France, Germany and the Low Countries, that same contemplative ideal was carried forward by a group called the "Recollects."

In France the houses of recollection spread slowly at first— the Wars of Religion in the 1500s impeded the urgent task of reform in the French provinces of the Observants. At a General Chapter in Paris (1579) the Minister General, Francesco Gonzaga, urged the foundation of houses of recollection but to little effect. He took special interest in a group of friars who had joined the Capuchin Reform in their search for a more eremitical form of life and had later returned to the Observants. He granted them houses to be formed into a Custody. They, after the example of the Reformed, Discalced and Capuchin friars, adopted the poor habit with a small hood, considered the original form of the friars' habit.[53]

---

52   *Ibid.*, p. 180.

53   *Ibid.*, p. 181.

Under pressure from Clement VIII to address the problem of reform movements, the Minister General, Bonaventura da Caltagirone, gave the French and Belgian houses of recollection their first statutes in 1597 while assuring that they remained under the authority of the Observant superiors.

With the support of the king and enjoying great prestige among all classes of society, the houses of recollection spread throughout France in the early 1600s, and the friars associated with them became known as Recollects. They modified the habit by their use of a hood shaped like an inverted pyramid, but in their style of life strongly resembled the other reform groups of their day, the Discalced, Reformed and Capuchins.[54]

During the early 1600s a Recollect Province was founded in Flanders. In 1621 the German friars of Cologne accepted the Recollect program for all their houses and in 1646 officially declared themselves Recollects. In 1670 Lower Germany followed suit, and by 1682 all the Provinces of Germany and Flanders had become Recollect. By the end of the seventeenth century the Recollects could claim four hundred houses with some ten thousand friars.[55]

The Capuchins

The action of Leo X in 1517, separating Observants and Conventuals, confirmed the ascendancy of a reformed movement that had already become an institution within which a new wave of reform was gathering momentum. In 1525 that wave broke with the flight of a friar from the house at Montefalcone, in the Province of the Marches, in the rugged country rising from north-

---

54   Ibid.

55   Ibid., p. 229

central Italy's Adriatic Coast. A young friar, ordained, but with scarce education, Matteo da Basci, wished to promote a reform of the Franciscan life: to observe the *Rule* literally and to adopt a habit like that of Francis himself— with a cone-shaped hood attached to the tunic (similar to that adopted by the Discalced friars in Spain).[56]

Without informing his superiors whom he presumed would disapprove, he fled to Rome and received oral approval of his plan from Pope Clement VII. Later imprisoned by his Minister Provincial for being "a fugitive and a vagrant," he was released through the intervention of his powerful protectress, the Duchess Caterina Cybo of Camerino, niece of the Pope.[57]

Others were soon to join Matteo in his quest for a reformed life. Two blood brothers, Ludovico and Raffaele, resided in the friary of their hometown, Fossombrone, in the Province of the Marches. Nourishing a desire to live a reformed life, Ludovico spoke with his Provincial Minister during an encounter there in 1526. He asked for permission to retire to a little house where he and others could live a secluded and reformed life: otherwise he would join Matteo. The minister, Giovanni da Fano, responded to his request by having him locked up in a cell of the friary. The next day Ludovico was gone (either released or escaped) and reached Matteo at the town of Montefeltro. Matteo informed him that he had no authority to admit others to his way of life; only the Pope could take that action. Ludovico procured letters of introduction from Matteo's benefactress, the Duchess Catherine, and made his way to her uncle at Rome. There he received the necessary papal permission for himself and his brother Raffaele to retire to

---

56   D'Arquata, p. 13.

57   *Ibid.*, p. 14.

a solitary house near Cingoli to live as hermits.[58]

Giovanni, the Minister of the Province, zealous but imprudent in his desire to thwart division in the Order, was determined to capture these rebels. Unsuccessful at Rome in his purpose of gaining an abrogation of the papal permission, he did obtain permission from the Cardinal Chief Penitentiary to "imprison even with the help of the secular arm, some apostate Religious who, with protection, wander around the Province, trying to form a faction." At Giovanni's orders, a group of soldiers and friars set out on an expedition to the hermitage at Cingoli.[59]

Ludovico had been a soldier before joining the Order, and he now put his military training to good use. Informed by a local farmer of the posse's arrival, Ludovico, his brother and their informant staged a successful ruse. Rushing back and forth through the house in order to appear numerous, clanking chains and metal pots, barking orders for the defense of the house against intruders, they frightened off the expedition that expected to find only two defenseless friars in the house.

The two brothers left their temporary refuge at Cingoli that same night obtaining refuge with the Camaldolese monks nearby at Massaccio. Undaunted, the Minister sent out another posse to arrest them there. Ludovico this time agreed to surrender, but only in the presence of the Pope's Delegate at Macerata. Once there, he displayed the still valid papal permission he received and the Delegate allowed him to return to his Camaldolese hosts. The Abbot there recommended to him the hermitage of Pascilupo at Albacina and wrote a letter of introduction for him addressed

58   *Ibid.*, p. 15.

59   *Ibid.*, p. 16.

to the community of a monastery nearby.[60]

Once again Ludovico and Raffaele set out but were no sooner safely established at Albacina than the Minister sent fourteen armed friars to arrest them. Informed by one of the monks living nearby, the brothers lit a bonfire in front of the hermitage, burning torches in all the windows and a signal-fire on the large rock guarding the entrance. Once again, with commands echoing from different corners of the hermitage, the arresting party was scared away.

The two would-be reformers moved again, this time to a house belonging to their family near their home in Fossombrone. There Matteo da Basci visited them in the company of Paolo da Chiozza, another friar who had received papal permission to join them. As they were sitting down to their midday meal, twelve soldiers accompanied by two friars approached the house. Ludovico barricaded the door and the two brothers with their guests donned hats they found there, running from window to window shouting orders. Once again the posse retreated.[61]

The four decided that to solve their problem with the Minister, Giovanni, they should put themselves outside his authority by requesting acceptance by the Conventual friars. After conferring with the Duke and Duchess of Camerino, they were sent to the local bishop who concurred with the wisdom of their decision. The Conventual Provincial Minister agreed, and the Conventual General gave his assent to the proposal. Finally the Pope approved the plan with the Bull *Religionis zelus* (July 3, 1528).[62]

The four companions found a home near Camerino and soon

---

60   *Ibid.*

61   *Ibid.*, p. 17.

62   *Ibid.*, p. 18.

welcomed other Observant friars to their community so that by April of 1529 they counted four houses and held their first chapter at Albacina. There the twelve chapter members drew up their Constitutions and elected Matteo their Vicar General, under the obedience of the Conventual Minister General. A group with similar aspirations, living in Calabria, was joined to them that summer.

This was the birth of the Friars of the Eremitical Life who, in 1532, officially adopted their nickname of "little hoods," *Cappuccini* or Capuchins. They remained, nominally, a part of the Conventuals until 1619 when they became fully independent with their own Minister General.[63]

With the independence of the Capuchins, the First Order, the Lesser Brothers or Friars Minor, took on the general institutional form which has continued to this day, one Order in three Orders: the Order of Friars Minor Conventual, the Order of Friars Minor (Observants), and the Order of Friars Minor Capuchin. Each traces its history back to the earliest days of the fraternity, and each shows, in different ways, the results of the long struggles of reform and division that have characterized the Lesser Brothers from their beginnings.

---

63   *Ibid.*

3

The Poor Sisters: Growth and Reform[1]

The Lesser Brothers have experienced both growth and reform during their history. It is now time for us to examine those phenomena in the life of the Poor Sisters, the family of Saint Clare.

Clare had lived at San Damiano for forty-three years, until her death in 1253. Her sisters left their original home in 1260, moving into new quarters within the city walls, at what is known today as the Proto-Monastery, attached to the Basilica of Saint Clare. As a reminder of their early home they took with them the crucifix from the chapel of San Damiano, a reminder also of the experience of Francis himself, who heard when praying before that crucifix the command to repair Christ's church.[2]

Like the Lesser Brothers, the Poor Sisters knew their Golden Age during the first fifty years of their existence. By the time of Bonaventure's death in 1274, they had entered a period of

---

1 I am indebted here to the study of Alberto Ghinato, L'Ideale di Santa Chiara attraverso i secoli," in *Santa Chiara d'Assisi Studi e Cronaca del VII Centenario* (Assisi: Comitato Centrale per il VII Centenario [della] Morte [di] s. Chiara, 1954), pp. 313-337.

2 *Ibid.*, p. 314.

declining fervor.[3]

During the next century the problems centered around dispensations from strict poverty, the appearance of a certain luxury of life and, accompanying these, a gradual relaxation of the practice of enclosure. For the many communities who followed the *Rule* published by Pope Urban IV, the monastery itself could own property, yet it seems that some sisters also accepted payment of personal rents, a practice strictly forbidden by the Rule. While problems regarding poverty multiplied, a steady stream of ladies of the nobility joined what was now called the "Order of St. Clare." Some sources indicate that individual monasteries even made nobility a condition for acceptance to the community.[4] Scandals arose as more and more frequently the sisters received permission to leave the monastery for briefer or longer periods, and "Poor Ladies" were brought to live as "contemplatives in residence" at the royal courts of Europe.[5]

The Poor Sisters soon came to know the dynamic of reform, as the fifteenth century brought them, like the Lesser Brothers, to a desire for a "stricter observance" of their several *Rules*. Such renewal in the women's monasteries often coincided with similar movements among the Lesser Brothers. In the 1400s the Observant reform among the Lesser Brothers in Italy began to affect women's communities as well. Leaders of the Observants, Bernardine of Siena, Bernardine of Feltre, and John Capistran, were at first unenthusiastic about a program of reform in the women's communities but, under pressure from the Holy See, began to spread their ideas in the monasteries. The monasteries

---

3   *Ibid.*, p. 322.

4   See G. Duchesne, *Histoire de l'abbaye royale de Longchamp* (1906), p. 23.

5   Ghinato, p. 324.

of Santa Lucia (Foligno), Sant'Orsola (Milan), Corpus Domini (Mantova), and the monastery of Ferrara became centers for a renewed "observance" among the Poor Sisters in Italy.[6]

Colette of Corbie and Her Reform

In France an even more significant reform began among the Poor Sisters. Its leader, Nicolette ("Colette") Boellet of Corbie, was born in 1381, daughter of a carpenter in the Picardy region.[7] In 1406 Colette received permission from Pope Benedict XIII to undertake a reform of the three Orders of the Franciscan Family, a reform whose impact was felt most strongly in the Order of St. Clare, the Poor Sisters. Unsuccessful in her attempt to bring reform to the monastery of her native Corbie, she finally succeeded in 1410 with the reform of the monastery at Besançon. Over the next three decades she founded sixteen houses where the reform took root. Her sisters, sometimes called "the savages of Le Puy" because of their austerity, were noted for their firm refusal of property ownership, whether individual or corporate, and for their emphasis on strict enclosure, excluding relations with the secular world.[8]

A highly intelligent and decisive leader, Colette usually received what she requested from popes, kings, princes and prelates. Her careful supervision of the building of a monastery for her sisters at Auxonne made her seem a professional builder

---

6   *Ibid.*, pp. 326-327.

7   For information on St. Colette I am indebted to Marie Richards of the Department of History of the University of California at Berkeley, who kindly supplied me with materials she has collected for her doctoral dissertation: *Franciscan Women: The Colettine Reform of the Order of Saint Clare in the Fifteenth Century* (University of California, Berkeley, 1989).

8   Ghinato, p. 327.

who had learned the craft of her carpenter father.[9] She moved easily through the territory of opposing factions in the bloody upheavals of The Hundred Years' War. Bands of mercenaries that roamed through France at that time respected the coach of this revered Abbess of Besançon. Her action paralleled that of Joan of Arc and, according to legend, when Colette passed through the French heroine's hometown of Domremy, she blessed the infant Joan.

Colette's action extended beyond the Order of St. Clare to the reform of communities of Lesser Brothers as well. John Capistran invited Colette to ally herself with the Observant Movement he was promoting so vigorously among the friars. Colette preferred to associate with the friars of the Community, the Conventual branch of the friars, among whom her influence stimulated a reform, that of the Colettan friars. In 1517, at the division of the Order decreed by Pope Leo X, Colette's followers, the Colettine Poor Sisters, were affiliated to the Observant friars by papal decree. By the end of the fifteenth century the Colettines had communities in practically all the principal cities of France while new foundations appeared in Belgium and England. Soon they also established themselves in the Americas.[10]

New Reforms in Spain and Italy

In 1480 a new branch of the Franciscan Family appeared in Spain with the founding of the Nuns of the Conception of the Blessed Virgin Mary by Beatrice de Silva. Though originally following the Rule of the Cistercian nuns, the Conceptionists

---

9   See Mother Mary Francis, P.C.C., *Walled in Light: St. Colette* (Chicago: Franciscan Herald Press, 1959), p. 124.

10   Ghinato, p. 327.

in 1520 received the privileges accorded by the Holy See to the Lesser Brothers and Poor Sisters. Some of them in fact adopted the *Rule* of St. Clare under the guidance of the Franciscan Cardinal Francisco Ximenes.[11]

In Italy a renewal allied to that of the Observant friars took root among the Poor Sisters. Caterina de' Vigri, of a noble family of Ferrara, entered the women's community of the Third Order Regular in her home town at the age of fourteen. This monastery, like many others in Italy and elsewhere, under the influence of the Observant friars, adopted the *Rule* of St. Clare in 1434. In 1456 Catherine was elected abbess of a new foundation, the monastery of Corpus Domini in Bologna, and soon attracted some two hundred women to the new community there. (Because of the importance of her work there, she is known today as Saint Catherine of Bologna.) In the midst of this burgeoning community of reformed life Catherine produced an impressive series of literary works on the spiritual life.[12]

Her contemporaries, also Poor Sisters dedicated to scholarship and writing, included Agnes de Haricuria who wrote a *Life* of Isabel of France, the foundress of the French reform at Longchamp. Illuminata Bembo wrote Catherine's own *Life*, and Perrine de la Baume et la Roche composed the *Life* of Colette of Corbie. In Sicily, Giacoma Policina and Cecilia and Girolama da Messina published works exalting the saintly Eustochia of Messina. Battista Varani composed several volumes of *Meditations* during this period, revealing the deep attachment of the Poor Sisters to reflection on the suffering of Christ.[13]

---

11   *Ibid.*, pp. 327-328.

12   *Ibid.*, p. 328.

13   *Ibid.*, p. 329.

Besides giving to the Franciscan world works of biography and spirituality, the family of St. Clare also produced historians in the fifteenth century. We may mention Alessandra of Foligno, Cecilia Coppoli and Eufrasia Alfari of Perugia, chroniclers of the life of the Poor Sisters in Umbria. The *belles-lettres* and poetry had their exponents in Battista da Montefeltro, Isabella Farnese and Girolama of Castille.[14]

Expansion Outside Europe

Having spoken of reforms among the Poor Sisters in the first three centuries of their existence, it may be well at this point to note the geographical expansion of the Order of Saint Clare. New foundations were being made, not only in the countries of Europe, but far beyond its borders, even to the lands discovered by Europeans during the "Age of Discovery."[15]

Clare herself, like Francis, had a keen interest in the Holy Land which, during her lifetime, was the scene of the Crusades. The breviary of St. Francis, carefully guarded at the Proto-Monastery in Assisi, includes a prayer for the freedom of the Holy Places in Palestine.[16]

During Clare's life, or shortly after her death, the Poor Sisters had made a foundation in the Near East. A letter of Pope Alexander IV dated 1257 grants privileges to the monastery of Poor Sisters at Antioch in Syria. Sources also indicate that the sisters of that community were killed during the Islamic invasion of 1268. We

---

14   *Ibid.*

15   Information on geographical expansion is taken from Berardo Capezzali, "Le Clarisse in terra di missione," in *Santa Chiara d'Assisi*, pp. 495-99.

16   See Ignacio Omaecheverria, *Chiara d'Assisi: Ressegna del Protomonastero*, vol. II, no. 2 (1954), p. 55, quoted in Capezzali, p.495.

know that in 1291, during the invasion of Islamic forces at Acre in Palestine, seventy-four Poor Sisters lost their lives there.[17]

At Tripoli, in modern day Libya, a famous monastery dedicated to St. Clare was destroyed during the invasion of 1289. The Abbess, named Lucia, and other sisters suffered death at the hands of Islamic troops. In Cyprus, the monastery of St. Clare was founded at Nicosia sometime before 1290, and another house, that of Santa Maria di Cava began in the early fourteenth century. It survived until the time of the Turkish invasion in the 1470s. Other monasteries of Poor Sisters disappeared during the same turbulent years: Caffa in the Crimea, and Chania and Candia on the island of Crete.[18]

Poor Sisters and Lesser Brothers

The problems of the friars' assistance of the women's communities appeared again in the 1500s with the ruling of the Minister General, Lichetto, that any new monastery must have the means to support at least fifty nuns (1518) and the decision of the General Chapter (1532) that excluded economic dependence of the women on the men's communities. The Council of Trent made a similar ruling that each monastery must have sufficient resources to support the community. The Colettines in particular opposed these rulings as contrary to their spirit and practice.

While the issue of economic assistance lay beneath these discussions, friars still offered spiritual assistance to the monasteries. Guidelines for this ministry were given by the Minister General Francesco Gonzaga (1582) and by the General

---

17   Capezzali, p. 496.

18   *Ibid.*

Chapters of Valladolid (1593) and Rome (1639).[19]

In several countries the Poor Clares suffered during the Protestant Reformation. The case of the monastery at Nuremberg is particularly poignant. The ancient, famous monastery, first Augustinian, passing to the *Rule* of St. Clare in 1274, counted some sixty members at the outbreak of the Reformation. The Abbess there since 1503 was a woman named Charitas Pirkheimer (b. 1466), an eminent humanist and a correspondent of Erasmus. Her father was an ambassador, her brother a friend of both Erasmus and Melancthon. She was an avid patristic scholar and liked especially to read Jerome. She participated actively in the theological debates of the time during the years of fierce disputes heralding the Protestant Reformation. Her community at Nuremberg had already received threats in 1522 from partisans of the Reformation because of the sisters' opposition to the Reformers' plans. On learning that the Abbess wrote to congratulate an author, Jerome Emser, who had criticized Luther, some of his supporters intercepted her letter and published it, setting in motion a persecution which soon led to the community's suppression.

The City Council, on learning of Charitas' views, stopped the subsidy of the monastery guaranteed at its foundation. The nuns were forbidden to communicate with the Franciscan friars, and were obliged, four times a week, to listen to the sermons of a city-appointed chaplain who attempted to convince the sisters to reject the religious life and embrace the Lutheran Reform. The sisters' use of the religious habit was forbidden and their practice of enclosure ignored. Charitas died in 1532, having seen members of the community forcibly removed from the cloister.

---

19   Ghinato, p. 330.

The monastery's numbers dwindled as sisters were removed or died without the hope of receiving new members. The last sister of the community died in 1591, having lived as a virtual exile for sixty years.[20]

Other communities of Poor Sisters suffered in the 1530s during the violent confrontations of the Reformation. At the monastery of Geneva the community was interrogated for ten hours about which of the sisters wished to leave the religious state and marry (only one young sister did). Expelled from their home, the community fled to France suffering the hardships recorded in the *Diary* of one of the sisters, Jeanne de Jussie. The monasteries of Vevey and Orbe were destroyed shortly thereafter, and many of the sisters fled to Evian in 1536. (In 1591 Evian itself was sacked, the monastery destroyed and the community dispersed). The Huguenots in France sacked and destroyed the monasteries of Lezignan, Nevers, Gien, Montbrison, Grenoble, and Béziers which were abandoned more than once and then repaired and repopulated by Poor Clares.[21]

The Calvinists of the Low Countries called *Geuzen* attacked the convent of Bruges in 1572, and in 1577 burnt that of Ghent. The nuns of Delft in Holland fled to Lisbon for refuge, and the monasteries of Harlem and Amsterdam were razed. The Poor Clares were soon forced to flee England too, moving to the north of France and the Brabant for safety. English troops in the Caribbean in 1586 also destroyed the monastery of the Poor Clares in Haiti.[22]

But besides persecution and exile, the Poor Sisters during the sixteenth century also knew moments of brilliance, especially in

---

20   *Ibid.*, p. 333.

21   *Ibid.*

22   *Ibid.*, pp. 333-334.

works of their spiritual writers. Among the important figures of
the period we may note St. Veronica Giuliani. She was Abbess
of the Capuchin Poor Sisters' monastery at Città di Castello
north of Assisi. A mystic and a stigmatic, her ten volumes of
autobiographical writings reveal the spirituality behind many
of the reform movements of the time, especially an intense
attachment to the suffering Christ.[23]

The themes of mortification and penance expressed by
Veronica were notable in the life of such a spiritual leader as Maria
Maddalena Martinengo. Maria Angela Gini was distinguished
for her learning as was Firmina Cesi of Foligno "who knew Latin
like a University don."[24]

In Spain the doctrine of the Immaculate Conception attracted
women writers like Claudia de San Miguel who composed the
Glossa pro Immaculata Conceptione and Maria de Pernia who
wrote poems dedicated to the same doctrine. The "pious and
most learned" Stefania de la Incarnación produced volumes
of theological, philosophical and mystical works. Basing her
expositions on the teachings of John Duns Scotus, Venerable
Maria de Agreda produced her *magnum opus, The Mystical City of
God (La mistica ciudad de Dios).*[25]

---

23 See Piero Chiminelli, "Moderne Figure di Clarisse," in *Santa Chiara d'Assisi*, p. 501.
On Veronica and other important Poor Clare writers, see C.A. Lainati, *Temi spirituali degli scriitti del Second'Ordine francescano* (Santa Maria degli Angeli, Assisi: Edizioni Porziuncola, 1970) and I. Omaechevarria, *Las clarisas a traves de los siglos* (Madrid: Ediciones Cisneros. 1972.

24 Ghinato, p. 335.

25 *Ibid.*

Reforms of the Seventeenth Century

Another series of reforms affected both the Lesser Brothers and the Poor Sisters during the 1600s: Recollect, Alcantarine, Reformed and Capuchin friars recalled the example of Francis and earlier reformers, and often found allies for their causes in the women's monasteries. Thus we notice in France, alongside the Recollect friars, monasteries of Recollect Poor Sisters. The Alcantarine friars would find a female counterpart in the Discalced Poor Sisters, called Poor Clare Solitaries of St. Peter of Alcantara, established at Farfa in 1679. These women lived an eremitical life similar to that of Carthusian solitaries.[26]

A foundation of Capuchin Poor Sisters interpreted the Constitutions of the "beautiful and holy reform" for women's communities. Also called Daughters of the Passion, they were founded in 1538 at Naples by Venerable Maria Lorenza Longo, formerly a Third Order member, who adopted the *Rule* of St. Clare for her new community. The Capuchin Poor Clares spread throughout Italy, Spain, and France in the following years as the Capuchin friars expanded. These new members of the family of St. Clare were encouraged by Cardinal Barberini who also aided another foundress, Maria Francesca Farnese, in her foundation of the Poor Clares of the Strictest Observance at a monastery in Albano in the hills outside Rome.[27]

The so-called Royal Urbanists (referring to both their royal patronage and their following the *Rule* promulgated by Pope Urban IV) and other Urbanist reforms among Poor Sisters also grew in this period. The Royal Urbanists were particularly interesting: they abandoned the enclosure, common life and the

---

26   *Ibid.*, p. 331.

27   *Ibid.*

religious habit. They lived as noblewomen in private dwellings and travelled freely. They disappeared during the French Revolution.[28]

The Poor Sisters also took their form of life to Asia for the first time during the seventeenth century. In 1621 a group of sisters from the monastery of Toledo, Santa Isabel de los Reyes, arrived in the Philippine Islands. They settled in Manila where, until the first half of our own century, they would remain the only community of contemplative Christian women in the rich religious panorama of Asia. Six sisters from the Manila community travelled to Macao on the coast of China in 1634 to begin a new foundation there. They were allowed to remain there only ten years before they were expelled from the country and forced to return to Manila.[29]

The Poor Sisters in the Eighteenth Century

Religious life generally suffered doubly in the 1700s: from lack of vitality within and the hostility of the new secularism from without. Casting a glance backward, the statistician of religious orders could note that the sixteenth and seventeenth centuries saw a great increase both in the number of monasteries and in the number of Poor Sisters due in part to the activity and vitality of the new reform groups. Even when the Protestant Reformation had already closed many monasteries, in 1587 some six hundred monasteries still belonged to the Order of St. Clare. A century later in 1680 we see the zenith of the Order's numerical growth: 934 monasteries with 34,000 Poor Clares under the jurisdiction of the friars and perhaps that many again under the jurisdiction

---

28   *Ibid.*, p. 332.

29   Capezzali, p. 497.

of local bishops. This would make for a total of some 70,000 Poor Sisters at the end of the seventeenth century.[30]

In the early eighteenth century the number of monasteries continued to increase while the number of nuns began to decline leaving many monasteries with small communities. As hostility toward religious became more apparent in mid-century, these small communities were the first targets of national governments anxious to close them and confiscate their property. These beginnings of suppression were soon followed by more general measures. Joseph II of Austria in 1781 decreed the suppression in his realm of monasteries without income. In 1782 the community of Ghent fled to France taking with them the body of St. Colette, and in 1783 the community of Bruges followed the same course of exile to France.[31]

The early eighteenth century saw the influence of Jansenism growing in religious communities in France. Poor Sisters were among those who vigorously rejected this doctrine. The Abbess of Lyon, Marie de St.Alexis (d. 1782) resisted her superior, the Jansenist Abbé de Montazet, who opposed the practice of daily Communion for the religious of the community. The community of Poligny in 1720 sent away their confessor who had become an adherent of Jansenism. The same sisters, in 1750, ignoring the recommendation furnished him by King Louis XV, refused hospitality to a Carmelite friar known to be a Jansenist.[32]

Besides the religious questions posed by Jansenism, France's religious history was soon to face the challenge of revolution. And the Revolution of 1790 brought with it new tragedies. Refusing to

---

30   Ghinato, p. 332.

31   *Ibid.*

32   *Ibid.*, p. 334.

take the Oath of Citizenship usually meant death, yet a Colettine of Le Puy responded to a magistrate: "I made my oath on the day of profession, I have no others to make." When the Mayor of Marseilles offered the Capuchin Poor Clares of that city a legal pension, they politely declined saying, "We do not need anything, since we know the gallows awaits those who refuse to take the Oath of Citizenship." The Poor Sisters of Amiens, invited by the National Assembly in 1790 to declare their revenues, responded with a courageous letter explaining their practice of poverty, free of any possessions whatsoever. Expelled from the monastery, they wandered from refuge to refuge trying to observe their life of prayer and work in their temporary shelters. The sisters of Alençon spent a year and a half in jail for their resistance to the demands of the new government and the remaining monasteries fell one by one: Bescançon, Poligny, Evian, Montbrison, Romans, Perpignan, Lyons, Paris, Tulle, Argentan, Limoges, Saint-Omer. At Valenciennes on October 23, 1794, Sister (Blessed) Josephine Leroux was executed, a victim of the Revolution's guillotine.[33]

Growth and Suffering in the Nineteenth Century

When Pope Pius VII canonized the Poor Clare reformer, Colette of Corbie on May 24, 1807, the Church also celebrated a new era of vitality among the Poor Sisters though hardships were destined to mark the nineteenth century as it had the eighteenth.

The community of Bruges was reassembled in 1806 and, in 1812, that of Ghent. In 1829, as freedom returned to Belgium, these two communities made their influence felt outside their own country. The Abbess of Bruges, M. Maria Domenica, not

---

33   *Ibid.*

unlike Colette herself in the extent of her program, supervised the foundation of fourteen communities during her lifetime: nine in Belgium, three in England, and one in France. France saw monasteries reappearing at Peronne, Amiens, Lovans, Cambrai, Montbris, Aurillac and Marseilles. These were functioning already in 1807. Shortly thereafter Leringes, Alençon, Perpignan and many others were either restored or founded. Toward the end of the century, in 1876, the monastery of Lourdes began making its own foundation in Canada in 1902.[34]

Early attempts to bring the life of the Poor Sisters to the United States ended in discouragement and failure. A foundation at Georgetown in 1792 under the Abbess Maria De Marche had survived for only fourteen years. Later unsuccessful attempts to establish the Franciscan women's contemplative life took them to Cincinnati (1826-28), Pittsburgh (1828-30), Detroit (1833-39), Green Bay (1833), and back to Pittsburgh (1835-39).[35]

Two blood sisters, both Poor Sisters, were responsible for establishing the first permanent community of the family of St. Clare in the United States. They were Mother Maria Maddalena and Sister Costanza of the noble family of the Bentivoglio of Bologna. At the encouragement of the Observant Minister General, Bernardino of Portogruaro, they set out from the Roman monastery of San Lorenzo in Panisperna, arriving in the U.S. in August of 1875. The two sisters also knew disappointment at first, failing to find in the American Church either support for a contemplative community or even understanding of it. They travelled from Cincinnati to Philadelphia, then south to New Orleans, and north again to Cleveland before finding a home in

---

34   *Ibid.*, p.335.

35   Chiminelli, p. 503.

Omaha, Nebraska. A layman, John Creighton, furnished a home for them there in 1878 and even rebuilt it after it was destroyed by a storm. The Omaha monastery was solemnly blessed in 1882. Before her death in 1905, Mother Maddalena had made three foundations from the Omaha monastery. [36]

Other pioneering Poor Sisters moved from the French monastery of Paray-le-Monial to establish a foundation at Nazareth in 1884. There Charles de Foucauld found work and a temporary home in 1897. The following year Charles, "the Poor Clares' hermit," moved to the Jerusalem monastery which had opened in 1888.

Two sisters from the Jerusalem community founded a new monastery near Alexandria, Egypt, during the community's exile from Jerusalem during World War I.[37]

The Twentieth Century

Though at the beginning of the Twentieth century the Poor Sisters still encountered numerous difficulties, they could still count some five hundred monasteries and approximately 10,000 members of the Order of St. Clare. Their growth may be attributed to the growth of the Poor Sisters in "mission territories" during this time.[38]

Pope Pius XI in 1929 had called for the presence of contemplatives in the "missions" and received a generous response from the followers of St. Clare. In keeping with an ancient Franciscan tradition, they set out almost immediately for an Islamic nation. Three nuns from Bordeaux in France set out in

---

36   *Ibid.*, p. 504.

37   Capezzali, p. 497.

38   Ghinato, p. 336.

1930 to start a community in Morocco, at Casablanca. Others in North Africa followed soon after, at Algiers in 1932 and Rabat in 1935.

The Colettine nuns from Besançon in France began a long and dangerous search for a home in Southeast Asia in 1932. They settled first at Pegu in the south of Burma. The outbreak of World War II forced them to seek refuge in Mandalay with the Franciscan Missionaries of Mary there. In their search for a refuge, they travelled on to India where they stayed first in Calcutta, then in the foothills of the Himalayas in a Jesuit house. The Capuchin friars offered them a home at Alwaye in Malabar where their decade of wandering ended with the establishment of a monastery in 1942.[39]

The war had brought suffering to other Franciscan women, too. Dutch Poor Sisters had made their foundation in Java at Tjitwing in 1934. With the outbreak of hostilities, they were interned and their monastery nearly destroyed. In 1936 Capuchin Poor Sisters from Florence, Italy, made their first foundation at Banpong in Thailand. In the same year the monastery at Vinh, Vietnam, began. Though Capuchin Poor Sisters from Holland had set out to make a foundation in Borneo in 1937, the war and its aftermath prevented them from realizing their project until 1950.[40]

In Japan, Poor Sisters from the monastery of Valleyfield, Canada, formed their first community shortly after the war, in 1947 at Denenchofu. The monastery of Nishinomiya, especially founded for Japanese women, opened in 1949.

Australia soon saw the beginnings of another community founded by Poor Sisters from the monastery of Galway, Ireland.

39   Capezzali, p. 497.

40   *Ibid.*

In 1951 they founded their house at Waverley, near Sydney.[41]

The development of new women's communities among the Poor Sisters has also marked this century. Some communities of enclosed nuns, choosing to undertake an active apostolate, became a different kind of religious family. While professing the Poor Sisters' *Rule* (that of St. Clare or of Pope Urban), they established a form of life without papal enclosure and with a model of centralized government for the various houses rather than the model of autonomous monasteries. The Irish Poor Clares of the Immaculate Conception of the Dublin monastery chose such a form of life as early as 1807 and have continued in this new style to this day. The Poor Sisters of the monastery of Cuernavaca made a similar move becoming the Missionary Poor Clares of the Blessed Sacrament, officially recognized in 1945. They were responsible for founding a community in Tokyo, Japan, in 1952 dedicated to the work of evangelization.

The renewal of religious life in the years following the Second Vatican Council has led the Poor Sisters, in their many different branches, to a renewed interest in their common origins and in the specifically Franciscan characteristics of their contemplative life. Through the work of strengthening federations of monasteries and revising Constitutions to express their heritage in the contemporary Church, the sisters of St. Clare continue to provide a vital component to the Franciscan Family worldwide.

---

41   *Ibid.*, p. 498.

4

Brothers and Sisters of Penance

After examining the story of reform and division among the Poor Sisters and Lesser Brothers, we turn to the story of the Brothers and Sisters of Penance, or the Third Order. Just as the friars and Poor Sisters had seen the character of their Order change with the demands of succeeding generations, the Order of Penance experienced its own evolution, gradually dividing it into two major bodies, one of them for lay men and women and the other for men and women wishing to live a new form of religious life. This change would give rise to new names, Third Order Secular and Third Order Regular, identifying two differing styles of living the *Rule* of the Brothers and Sisters of Penance.[1]

Lay and Religious

In the thirteenth century, the Brothers and Sisters of Penance had among their members those who wanted to live their

---

1   Special attention is given to the development of women's congregations of the Third Order Regular in Pierre Peano, "Sisters of the Franciscan Order: Origins, History and Permanent Values" (Manuscript, n.d.). See also Raffaele Pazzelli, *The Franciscan Sisters: Outlines of History and Spirituality* (Steubenville, OH: Franciscan University Press, 1993).

penitential life in community and profess religious vows of poverty, chastity and obedience. Many of them also wished to combine their life of community with work, especially the service of lepers and the sick poor. They did not develop a new religious *Rule* (the Fourth Lateran Council had forbidden new *Rules*) but committed themselves to observing the "form of life" of the Brothers and Sisters of Penance while adding the distinctive note of living it *together*. They were exploring a new form of religious life, one that combined traditional elements of community life and prayer with the organized service of the needy.[2]

Those who promoted this new vision were encouraged by the revision of the Penitents' *Rule* published by Nicholas IV in 1289. This new *Rule* called the Brothers and Sisters Franciscan Tertiaries and, while not speaking of religious vows, described their life in a way that made them resemble members of religious rather than secular communities. The practice of making vows of poverty, chastity and obedience grew among some tertiaries and, despite early opposition, their initiative received official approval from Pope John XXII in 1323.

Pope John's action recognized the dual character of the Third Order: the tertiaries included lay men and women, "those who live in their own homes," and those who live in community making religious vows, while still professing the same *Rule*.

Communities of women tertiaries had already formed during the thirteenth century in France, Germany and Italy. In Belgium and Holland similar groups existed, and these multiplied as Beguines in those countries accepted the Tertiary Rule of Nicholas IV in order to protect themselves from ecclesiastical and civil persecution as heretics. These communities were independent

2   Iriarte, p. 581.

and non-cloistered, dedicated to apostolic work among the poor and the sick.

Saint Elizabeth of Hungary was considered a model by many of these groups. In 1228 she made a profession of life: to renounce the world and her own will, and to distribute her goods to the poor in founding a hospital. Elizabethines and Hospital Sisters or Gray Sisters in the thirteenth century followed her example, founding and living near hospitals in Germany, France and Belgium.[3]

In the fourteenth century another model emerged in Italy, that of cloistered, contemplative communities following the tertiary *Rule*. Angelina da Marsciano (d. 1435) founded such a community, the Monastery of Sant'Anna at Foligno near Assisi. Other monasteries of the same type were founded and organized themselves as members of a single family. They elected a General Minister in a General Chapter every three years and instituted a system of General Visitation of the houses.[4]

In the fourteenth century the lay Penitents suffered from the suspicion of heresy raised in their regard by those (especially some French bishops) who considered them to be like the Beghards, Beguines and Fraticelli condemned by the Council of Vienne in 1312.[5]

Coupled with this form of persecution came the huge losses of life inflicted by the plague, and the disarray provoked in every sector of Church life by the Great Western Schism. These combined to reduce notably the number of Penitents.

Toward the end of the fourteenth century, in 1385, a statistic notes that the Lesser Brothers served 244 fraternities of the

---

3   *Ibid.*

4   *Ibid.*, p. 584.

5   *Ibid.*, p. 561.

Brothers and Sisters of Penance, of which 141 were in Italy and the Orient, 23 in Spain, 29 in France, 37 in Germanic countries and 8 in the British Isles.[6]

Organization and Expansion

The communities of enclosed, contemplative tertiaries remained, and during the fifteenth century many of those following this life with solemn vows and strict enclosure became Poor Sisters' communities.

The tertiary communities who professed religious vows and worked in apostolic endeavors without enclosure formed "federations," "congregations," or "chapters" with each community retaining its autonomy. In the fifteenth century the Belgian Congregation of Zepperen united groups on this model, and the Dutch Chapter of Utrecht in 1439 linked seventy groups of Franciscan men and women religious who elected their own Minister General.[7]

This new style of federated communities soon began to develop in other countries as well. Some twenty years after the approval of the Flemish Congregation's statutes, the Spanish Congregation of men's communities received papal authorization to make solemn religious vows. With a Bull of 1447, Pope Nicholas V attempted to unite the numerous men's communities in Italy in a single Congregation with its own General Chapter and Minister General. He failed in the attempt, faced as he was with strong opposition from many communities who feared a loss of autonomy from such a step. The differing allegiances the many communities had upheld during the Great Schism made the

6   *Ibid.*, p. 562.

7   *Ibid.*, p. 583.

climate unfavorable toward projects of unification.

Official recognition of the permanent character of the religious profession made by the tertiaries' communities came toward the end of the century. Sixtus IV, in 1480, decreed that the vows of both men's and women's communities of the Third Order Regular should be considered as solemn vows, thus recognizing them as "true" religious in the Church.[8]

The fifteenth century saw a resurgence of the lay Penitents, especially under the leaders of the Observant movement, Bernardine of Siena, John Capistran, and Bernard de Bustis. The Dominican theologian, St. Antonine of Florence (d.1459), describes the Dominican tertiaries of his day as being relatively few in Italy and mostly women, while those "under the habit and rule of the Third Order of St. Francis" were numerous, both men and women, "some living as hermits, others as hospitallers, and still others grouped in congregations."[9]

During the following century, despite losses in some countries caused by the Reformation, the Penitents flourished in others. In the realms of Spain (including Naples, Lombardy, and Flanders), in Portugal, and in their territories in the Americas and Asia, the Third Order fairly exploded: it was considered "chic" for the upper classes and the object of a program of mass enrollment of the faithful. In 1586 it was estimated that more than 100,000 tertiaries were enrolled overseas.[10]

At this time Julius II modified the traditional, severe tunic and cord of the Tertiaries, considered excessive for members of the upper classes, and clumsy for working people, to a scapular

---

8   *Ibid.*, p. 585.

9   *Ibid.*, p. 562.

10   *Ibid.*, p. 587.

of two long woolen panels covering the chest and back, tied at the sides with a cord, all of which could be worn under ordinary clothing. (Clement XI in 1704 reduced it further to two small pieces of cloth and a detached cord.)[11]

Leo X and Third Order Religious

Leo X, in 1521, urged a union of Third Order Religious by promulgating a *Rule* for all the men's and women's communities. Adapting the ancient *Rule* of Nicholas IV of 1289 to the pattern of community life and adding new statutes, the Leonine *Rule* included the new feature of the profession of three solemn vows. The provision for strict enclosure of women's communities, while affirmed in the rule, allowed for a certain elasticity in practice since the needs of charitable works were to be taken into account. In the mid-1500s the Elizabethines or Sisters of Mercy, for example, were free of enclosure since they were dedicated to hospital care. They numbered nearly 4,000, especially numerous in France, Germany and Austria. With a distinctly Franciscan spirit and following the Rule of the Third Order of Saint Francis, Angela Merici (d. 1540) founded the Company of Saint Ursula which became a religious order only long after Angela's death.[12]

Among the men Penitents, examples of institutes dedicated to charitable works included the "Minims" or "Least Brethren" of Spain and Portugal dedicated to the service of the indigent sick. Founded in 1566 they were also known as *Obregones* after the name of their founder, the layman Bernardino Obregon. A community with a similar form of apostolate was that of the French tertiaries called the *Bons-Fils*. At Paris the "Gray Penitents"

---

11   *Ibid.*, p. 568.

12   *Ibid.*, p. 591.

dedicated themselves to educating young men from poor families as candidates for the priesthood.[13]

The *Rule* of Leo X did not provide for General Superiors: these were to be the Provincial Ministers of the First Order and their appointed Visitors. Here the Observant superiors demonstrated their wish that there should not be another Franciscan Order with its own central government like that of the First Order.

The Congregations of Spain and Lombardy, however, already had an autonomous existence with their respective central governments. The Spanish Congregation received in 1547 a set of three *Rules* from Paul III: one for the brothers living in community, one for nuns of enclosed life, and a third for lay persons living in their own homes or as hermits and recluses. Those professing any one of the three *Rules* were under the authority of the Minister General of the brothers' community. This system was to apply to the dominions of Spain and Portugal including the East and West Indies (Asia and the Americas).[14]

In Italy the greater number of communities joined the powerful Congregation of Lombardy which received full autonomy in 1549 with its own provincial and general superiors. Some twenty years later Pius V directed in 1568 that all the communities of men and women should be under the authority of the Observant superiors, and that all the women's communities should make profession of solemn vows and observe strict enclosure. Another two decades passed before Sixtus V granted the Tertiary communities relative autonomy. They were to elect their own Visitor General every three years in their own General Chapter. The Visitor General would govern the Congregation as a true religious superior, but

---

13   *Ibid.*, p. 586.

14   *Ibid.*

the Minister General of the Observants would keep the right to confirm the Visitor General's election and to visit all the Tertiary houses every five years (a practice that fell quickly into disuse).[15]

After the Council of Trent

Following the Council of Trent, Pius V in 1566 forbad women's communities which do not have solemn vows and strict, papal enclosure and, in 1568, decreed the outright suppression of all such groups then existing, forbidding that any others should be formed in the future. These severe measures would mark the history of Franciscan tertiary communities for the next two hundred years.[16]

From the sixteenth to the eighteenth century the "new face" of Franciscan women's congregations would be that of cloistered nuns of completely contemplative life, following the *Rule* of the Third Order, originally for the secular Brothers and Sisters of Penance.

Projects with the aim of bringing greater uniformity and centralization to women's Tertiary communities proved difficult. Some communities were under the authority of a local bishop, some observing the *Rule* of Nicholas IV and others that of Leo X. Other communities were under the authority of the Observant superiors, and followed their own special general Constitutions. A third group, also numerous, were under the authority of the superiors of the men's Tertiary Congregations.

To show the diversity among the women's tertiary communities we may take the example of Belgium. In 1647 there were forty-six tertiary communities. Twelve of these were monasteries

---

15   *Ibid.*

16   Peano, p. 33.

observing strict enclosure and subject to the Observants. Thirty-four communities were actively engaged in charitable works, especially in hospitals. Despite the decree of the Council of Trent imposing enclosure on all women religious, at the insistence of local governments these Belgian tertiary sisters were dispensed from the law of enclosure.

New congregations founded in the sixteenth and seventeenth centuries following the Tridentine ruling belonged to a movement called that of the Stricter Observance, communities professing solemn vows and strict enclosure. One example of such a community was the Pfanneregg Reform founded in Switzerland in 1587 under the leadership of Elizabeth Spiltzlin (d.1611). Inspired by the Capuchin friar Ludwig of Einsiedeln, in 1591 they accepted the habit and the spirit of the Capuchin Reform, and many other communities in Switzerland and Germany allied themselves to this movement, so that by the end of the 1600s more than twenty monasteries belonged to this Congregation.[17]

In France, the Saint-Omer Reform was also inspired by the example of the Capuchins. Beginning at Bourbourg in 1614 and Saint-Omer in 1620, Françoise Taffin (d.1642) founded a congregation that later included fifteen monasteries in France, Belgium and Germany. In Italy a smaller reform along the same lines was begun in Genoa in 1690 by Benedetta Wanherten Viganega (d.1724).[18]

Strange as it may seem, congregations of this new type would eventually inspire the burgeoning of Franciscan communities in the nineteenth and twentieth centuries. Two congregations founded in the seventeenth century deserve special mention in

---

17   Iriarte, p. 588.

18   *Ibid*.

this regard, one from Belgium, the other from Germany.

The Recollectines were founded in 1623 by Jeanne Neerinckx following the lines of the Recollect reform. Though an enclosed, contemplative community, the "nuns of the Limburg Reform" staffed an internal school in the convent for girls and could leave the cloister to nurse the sick in their homes when asked. (These "social functions" of the Recollectines would spare them from some of the harsh suppressions of cloistered communities in the eighteenth century.) The Recollectine Penitents were spread through sixteen houses before the foundress' death in 1648.

In 1622, in Aachen, Germany, Apollonia Radermacher founded the Elizabethines along the lines of enclosed, contemplative life.

As the Neerinckx and Radermacher communities divided and subdivided, they would contribute many of the foundresses of the nineteenth century congregations in Belgium, Holland, Germany and Northern France: the Franciscan communities which would exercise the greatest influence on North America and Brazil in the future.

In the 1600s a renewal movement within the lay Brothers and Sisters of Penance received strong encouragement from the various branches of the First Order. The General Chapter of Toledo in 1633 urged the "restoration" of the Third Order according to the model of Spain. The friar-chaplains of the royal courts of Europe persuaded members of the ruling families to join and favor the development of the Third Order, especially in the courts of Austria, in Savoy, and among the Gonzagas.

Italy could boast during this century that every city had its own flourishing fraternity, and members of both ecclesiastical and secular aristocracies boasted of their membership in the Third Order. Italian Tertiaries founded and maintained charitable works, hospitals, orphanages, and soup kitchens for the poor. Under Philip III and Philip IV in Spain and Portugal an "incredible enthusiasm" for the Third Order leads to such statistics as these: in Lisbon, in 1644, more than 11,000 tertiaries belonged to fraternities in the city; and in Madrid, in 1689, the number of tertiaries was estimated to exceed 25,000.[19]

In France the Third Order had an important religious role, especially through special congregations, e.g., of the Most Blessed Sacrament. The Capuchin friars promoted the Third Order vigorously in France, including such important figures as Joseph du Tremblay, Leonard de Paris and Yves de Paris.

The Third Order in Belgium seems not to have become a popular movement, remaining almost exclusively the domain of the aristocracy. But enthusiasm for the Third Order could be felt in Germany, Ireland and England.

In the New World, we may note the important contribution of the *beatas*, tertiary women of Madrid dedicated to teaching, called by fray Juan de Zumarraga to Mexico City where they opened a school to instruct native children.[20]

The men's Congregation of France by the seventeenth century was larger than that of Spain, including seven provinces, after an intense period of reform under Vincent Mussar leading to their name of The Strict Observance. This Congregation was that which kept the closest ties with the First Order and preserved its own statutes along side the Rule of Leo X. The great historian of monastic-religious orders, Hippolyte Helyot (d.1716), was a member of this congregation.[21]

---

19   *Ibid.*, p. 569.

20   *Ibid.*

21   *Ibid.*, p. 586.

At the beginning of the seventeenth century, despite heavy losses during the Reformation, in Germany the Third Order Regular counted more than two hundred houses. In 1625 the Order as a whole was composed of seventeen provinces in 327 houses with 3,990 professed members. At the beginning of the 1600s thirty houses existed in Ireland.[22]

In 1700 France counted four Provinces, Spain and Portugal three, all of these dependent on the Minister General of the Friars Minor, with some one hundred houses and 1,761 religious. The whole of the Third Order Regular at that time numbered twenty provinces with over two hundred houses and nearly four thousand members.

While the beginning of the 1700s saw the Third Order flourishing, the second half of the century became the period of great testing for the Brothers and Sisters of Penance. In 1776 the Empress Maria Theresa of Austria forbad the acceptance of new members of the Third Order. Joseph II, in 1782, suppressed the Third Order in all its forms.[23]

France's "Civil Constitution of the Clergy" in 1790 suppressed the Third Order in that country, decreeing also the confiscation of all the fraternities' properties. Under Napoleon, in 1810, the Third Order was again declared suppressed, and any meetings of tertiaries strictly forbidden.

While the religious orders in Spain were suppressed, the tertiary fraternities continued to exist. Some flourished during this period and the majority survived. Italy's religious suppression did not mean the disappearance of the tertiary fraternities: they simply changed their juridical character becoming private

---

22   *Ibid.*, p. 587.

23   *Ibid.*, p. 572.

organizations.[24]

Lay and Religious in the Last Century [25]

On December 12, 1818, the body of Francis was rediscovered in the crypt of the Basilica of the Saint in Assisi. After fifty-two nights of secret digging by the Conventual friars with the permission of Pius VII, the body was seen for the first time since its being hidden there in 1230.

In a way, that event symbolically marks the rediscovery of Francis in the nineteenth century, a period that brought the Franciscans to an all-time low, and also saw the beginnings of their rebirth.

The Romantic Movement dominated the cultural scene during this century. The Romantics found in Francis a poet of nature, a sign of universal human brotherhood, a minstrel of God, and a witness to the dignity of labor. While the Romantics generally disdained members of religious orders, some exception was made for Franciscans.

In 1826 Josef Goerres published at Strasbourg his *Der Heilige Franziskus von Assisi. Ein Troubador.* This was an important work, marking the rediscovery of Francis as a poet. In the same year, 1826, Stendhal, the great master of the French novel, noted in one of his journals his admiration and respect for Francis.

Within a few years, on October 16, 1833, Chateaubriand wrote "The Social Impact of Franciscanism." Michelet, in his *Histoire de France*, proposed the figure of Francis as the antithesis of the official Church, opening the way to Protestant studies of Francis

---

24   *Ibid.*, pp. 571-572.

25   The materials on the nineteenth century Franciscan Movement can be found with greater detail in A. Gemelli, *Il Francescanesimo*, Chap. 7, whose work is summarized here.

as a rebel and reformer.

An early work by Montalembert (1836) entitled *St. Elizabeth of Hungary*, emphasized in its introduction the religious and civil work of the Franciscans in the thirteenth century.

Manzoni, the premier Italian writer of the end of the nineteenth and early twentieth centuries, wrote a "literary work marked by Franciscan spirituality," *I promessi sposi*.[26] The figure of Padre Cristoforo, the friar, forms that link with the Franciscan tradition as seen by the novelist Manzoni.

In 1847, Frederick Ozanam, professor at the Sorbonne, travelled to Assisi. He immediately took to Francis and translated Franciscan *laudes* and the *Fioretti* in his work on *Franciscan Poets in Italy*.[27] Affiliated to the Friars Minor, he went on to found the Society of St. Vincent de Paul to encourage the active collaboration of the laity in the service of the poor.

Karl von Hase, the year after Ozanam's death, wrote the *Franz vov Assisi* in which he presented his view of Francis as a pre-Protestant. Ernest Renan reviewed the work, and his studies led to the work of Paul Sabatier in the 1880s, marking a new beginning in the historical-critical study of Franciscan sources.

It was Paul Sabatier, with his *Vie de S. François* who founded, in the words of Masseron, a "Fourth Order" of "Franciscanophiles," intellectual and secular, that would multiply in the twentieth century.[28]

From the mid-1800s on, various factors conspired to help bring renewed prosperity to the lay Third Order: the restoration of the First Order in its various branches (with a more efficient and social

---

26   Gemelli, p. 318.

27   *Ibid.*, p. 323.

28   *Ibid.*, p. 354.

understanding of the apostolate and a clearer sense of specifically Franciscan methods of action), a wave of popular sympathy for St. Francis beginning in the intellectual circles of Europe, and the decisive support of several popes.

The Popes from Pius IX to John XXIII were members of the Third Order. Leo XIII especially promoted the tertiary life, both as Bishop of Perugia and as Bishop of Rome. For the Seventh Centenary of the birth of St. Francis in 1882, he praised the Third Order and strongly encouraged its diffusion in his letter *Auspicato concessum*. In 1884, he issued a revised *Rule* aimed at making the Third Order even more accessible to the masses of the faithful.[29]

The nineteenth century was ushered in with the religious persecution accompanying the French Revolution of 1790, followed soon after by the persecutions under Napoleon in 1803 and 1810. The suppression of religious orders was effected in Spain in 1820, renewed in 1831 and 1832 in Spain, Russia, Poland and Mexico. In 1866 religious orders were suppressed in Italy and their goods confiscated. A few years later the *Kulturkampf* in Bismarck's Germany did the same, as did Republican France. Between 1869 and 1880 several national governments tried to destroy religious.[30]

Using the principle that religious, to be tolerated, must perform some useful social function, national governments gave an impetus to the rise of a new type of religious congregation. The new congregations, many of them Franciscan, had no enclosure and professed simple vows, or were formed as a society without vows. These were dedicated to education, hospital work, missions and social assistance programs.

The nineteenth century, the most vocational of centuries,

---

29   Iriarte, p. 504.

30   Gemelli, p. 356.

witnessed the flourishing of new Franciscan women's communities. These institutes addressed the unmet social needs of the "new poor," the working classes of the Industrial Revolution.

The women's congregations of temporary or perpetual simple vows were not considered "religious" in the strict sense under Canon Law and thus were free to exercise an active ministry despite Trent's regulations on enclosure for religious women.[31]

The period from the middle of the nineteenth to the early years of the twentieth century saw the rise of more than two dozen Franciscan women's communities in the U.S. with ties to Europe. The burgeoning of religious communities in America in these years accompanied the expanding Catholic immigrant population, particularly the large Irish migration of the 1840s and 1850s, the German migration of the same period, followed by Eastern and Southern European immigrants, many of them Catholic from Italy and Poland in the 1880s and 1890s.

In many new foundations we see social needs of immigrant populations and struggles against anti-Catholic sentiment. The need for education, for Catholic schools, mandated by the Third Plenary Council of Baltimore (1884), set an agenda for local churches. For this reason many bishops and parish priests encouraged the foundation of new religious communities dedicated to this purpose. General needs for better health care facilities, both for Catholics and for the wider population, made work in medicine and nursing another pressing concern motivating the new congregations.

In 1849 a group of women and men, Franciscan secular

---

31   In the early 1900s the Holy See offered them "full citizenship" as religious, on the condition that they be "aggregated" to a religious order of solemn vows. Most Franciscan women's communities and some of the men's communities chose to accept this offer.

tertiaries, immigrants from Bavaria, proposed moving into the newly formed diocese of Milwaukee. The women founded the Franciscan Sisters of Penance and Charity under the leadership of Ottili Duerr Zahler (M. Emiliana). In the same year, 1849, in Glasgow, Scotland, Adelaide Vaast and Veronica Cordier founded the Franciscan Sisters of the Immaculate Conception. The following year, 1850, the Franciscan Sisters of the Immaculate Conception of Braintree, England, were founded by M. Elizabeth Lockhart and M. Frances Burton. These two communities would later inspire the beginnings of new communities in the United States.[32]

A young Franciscan tertiary nun from Vienna, Theresa Hackelmeier, founded the Franciscan Sisters of Oldenburg, Indiana, in 1851. In 1855, encouraged by their bishop, St. John Neumann, three Secular Franciscan Tertiaries, Anna Maria (Sr. Frances) Bachmann, Barbara (Sr. Margaret) Boll, and Anna (Sr. Bernardine) Dorn, founded the Franciscan Sisters of Philadelphia (Sr. Glen Riddle).

Further West, the Franciscan friar Pamfilo da Magliano invited a group of women to form a Franciscan congregation in Western New York. In 1859 two women from Philadelphia, Mary Joan Todd and Ellen O'Fallon, and soon after, Mary Ann O'Neil from Fort Lee, New Jersey, formed the beginnings of the Franciscan Sisters of Allegany. The assistance of a member of the young Philadelphia community, Sr. M. Michaela, helped them in their early formative period.

Alfreda Moes, encouraged by the same Pamfilo da Magliano, in 1865 founded the Franciscan Sisters of Mary Immaculate in

---

32   Information on each community is taken from the many articles on the individual congregations listed under "Francescane," in *DIP IV*.

Joliet, Illinois. The Joliet community in its turn gave rise to the Franciscan Sisters of Our Lady of Perpetual Help of St. Louis, Missouri in 1901. Moes, in 1878, moved to Rochester, Minnesota and founded the Franciscan Sisters of the Congregation of Our Lady of Lourdes. In 1916 this community gave the first members to the Franciscan Sisters of Our Lady of Lourdes of Sylvania, Ohio. During the 1860s the Philadelphia Franciscans formed two new communities in New York: the Franciscan Sisters of Syracuse, led by Bernardine Dorn, and those of Williamsville, under Margaret Boll.

With assistance from the Oldenburg community, in 1868 the first five sisters of the Franciscan Sisters of the Immaculate Conception of the Blessed Virgin Mary (of Clinton, Iowa) began the foundations of a new community near the Trappist Abbey of Gethsemani, Kentucky. In 1869, the Franciscan Sisters of Penance and Charity (Tiffin) were founded.

In 1871 the Franciscan Sisters of Perpetual Adoration were formed with a group which came from the Milwaukee community of 1849.

In the following year, 1872, the Franciscan Sisters of St. Mary began in St. Louis, Missouri.

Nearly a half-century earlier, in 1827, in Heythuizen, Holland, a young woman named Katrien Daemen had founded the Franciscan Sisters of Penance and Christian Charity. With the stormy religious conditions prevailing in Germany, a group of her sisters came to the U.S. in 1874. In the same year, a young German congregation, the Franciscan Sisters of the Holy Family, only ten years old, fleeing the *Kulturkampf* emigrated to the U.S., eventually making their headquarters in Dubuque, Iowa. This community, in 1877, spawned a new congregation, the Franciscan

Sisters of East Peoria, Illinois, encouraged by the pioneer bishop John Lancaster Spalding.

In 1874 another event linked European and American Franciscans. An English Franciscan, Elizabeth (Ignatia) Hayes, had been formed in the two Franciscan communities of the Immaculate Conception in Braintree, England, and Glasgow, Scotland. Vowing to be a missionary, Hayes came to the U.S. and founded the Missionary Franciscan Sisters of the Immaculate Conception in Belle Prairie, Minnesota in 1872.

This community would give rise to a series of new congregations as happened with the Philadelphia community and the Allegany and Joliet families. The Franciscan Sisters of Little Falls, Minnesota, began in 1890; in 1901 the Franciscan Sisters of the Immaculate Conception of Rock Island, Illinois, were founded.

In the same year the Englishwoman Hayes established Belle Prairie, 1872, a German woman, Anna Katherine Berger, founded the Franciscan Sisters of St. Mary, in St. Louis, Missouri. By 1894 a member of the St. Louis community, Maria Augustine Giesen, had founded a new congregation, the Franciscan Sisters of Maryville.

In Europe, new women's congregations emphasized the work of missionary evangelization. In 1877, Elena Chappotin de Neuville (Marie de la Passion) from Brittany founded the Franciscan Missionaries of Mary. They are today the largest of the Franciscan women's congregations.

The Turn of the Century

A movement for religious life in the Anglican Church during the later nineteenth century gave rise to two Franciscan communities including both men and women. The first, the Society of the Atonement, was founded by Father Paul Wattson and Mother Lurana Mary White in Graymoor, New York, in 1898.

In 1909, with fifteen of their followers, they were received into the Roman Catholic Church. The Apostolic Delegate to the United States at that time, Diomede Falconio, himself a Franciscan, assisted them. Soon after their reception, they affiliated with the Franciscan Family. The Society's commitment to service of the poor and their work for ecumenism have made them known to many in the U.S.

The other community is the Society of Saint Francis, sometimes known as the Anglican Franciscans. Divided into a First, Second and Third Order, the members of the community have become an outstanding sign of Franciscan values in the Anglican communion, especially in England and the U.S., favoring initiatives on behalf of the poor, the protection of creation, and for peace.

In the panorama of Franciscan congregations founded in the last century, the United States has been privileged to offer a home to many, some of them exiles, others children of immigrants. Their contributions to the life of the Church and society in this country have been notable. They have been instrumental in promoting much-needed social services, especially in education and health care for the poor. With them, other Franciscans enriched the American Church by their presence. Growing numbers of Friars Minor, Observant, Capuchin and Conventual came to serve the needs of the American Church. The number of Poor Clare monasteries grew and new foundations marked the "contemplative geography" of the North American continent. The numbers of the Brothers and Sisters of Penance (Third Order) expanded dramatically in the early years of this century as the importance of the laity in the Church was emphasized, and waves of immigration brought the traditions of European Franciscan laity to a new context.

Having surveyed the growth and development of the various branches of the Franciscans throughout their long history, it is now our task to examine their shared values and vision in an attempt to understand "what makes them tick." This task will lead us to consider their spirituality and some aspects of the life and work that flow from that religious vision of the world.

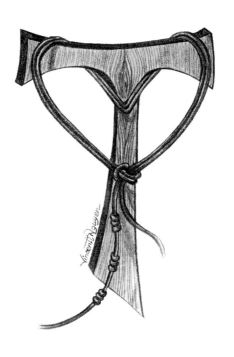

5

The Franciscan Spirit

If this work can be considered in some way a biography of the Franciscan Family, a description of that family would be incomplete if nothing were said about the spiritual environment in which it lives and grows and the climate it creates around itself. This chapter will describe characteristics, distinguishing features, special emphases of the Franciscan Family, and introduce the reader to some Franciscans who have helped to shape its spirit.

The Franciscans, in our great numbers and sometimes baffling diversity, hold in common a constellation of practices, ideas, devotions, and familiar images. All contribute to what may be called the "spirit" of Franciscans. In the following pages I will sketch outlines of this spiritual and intellectual topography.

A Poor Man's Theology

Francis was a theologian in the ancient sense, "one who speaks of God." Rarely expressed in dogmatic form, Francis' theology reveals itself in praises, letters, scraps of sermons, blessings, admonitions. Traits called characteristically and authentically Franciscan derive from this source. Over the centuries Francis' theological vision has received more systematic presentation in the works of such disciples as Bonaventure and John Duns Scotus. Here we will interweave pieces from various parts of the Franciscan theological tradition, presenting a rapid and necessarily incomplete picture of the kind of theology Francis expressed and inspired.

The God of Generous Love

God is good. Here is one possible beginning for Franciscan theology. God's goodness has special force because it is eminently real. The goodness of God the Creator (*fontalis plenitudo* for Bonaventure) is fully self-aware, this awareness being so real that it is personal and is called "the Word" (*exemplar omnium*). The bond between the fullness and the exemplar is likewise eminently real and personal, and is the Spirit (*cogeneratus*).

The very life of God is one of goodness expressing itself generously, fully. This divine goodness lives in personal communion. God is interpersonal and relational.

This communion has at its center the Word, the core or middle of God's life as Trinity. Wishing to express overflowing goodness, God wishes to pour out an expression of the divine life.

God's desire to share goodness is expressed as creation. But creation is not merely to receive some partial, limited sharing in God's goodness and life. God will actually give away even the very heart of the divine life, the Word.

With this in mind, the will to give away the very core of divine life, God forms the world through the Word. Since the Word will be the crowning glory of the creation, God makes light and darkness, trees, stones and fish, all the creatures, according to the Word as model or blueprint or form. The human person, man and woman, resembles most closely the model that God uses to create. Since the Word is to come among human beings as one of them, they resemble the Word very exactly.

In all this work of creation God shows one of the divine characteristics—outpouring of what is within, giving away all that is inside. This we may call the bowing over of God, the gesture typical of one who offers. We may also call this the humility of God, divine condescension. God gives away all, holds nothing back as property: this is the poverty of God, showing in the visible things of creation the invisible and constant self-giving which is the life of the Trinity. The world mirrors, now clearly, now obscurely, this inner, divine life of unending bowing over in generosity.

The universe and all creatures reflect God, speak of God, reveal God because they are made according to a pattern, the model of God's own heart, the core of the Trinity, the Word. The human person, coming at the completion of creation, gives voice to the praise of all creatures for the Creator.

The creation is fully understandable at the birth of Jesus. Here is the "missing link," always present, now visible. The core, the middle, the center of God's own inner communion comes in order to be a creature. With the coming of the Word as one of them, creatures find their model enfleshed. Christ is no alien in a strange universe: he was from the beginning the reason and the Creator's blueprint for every particle of matter, for all things visible and invisible, for everything and everyone.

Whatever is beautiful reflects his beauty; whatever is living, lives because of him; whatever is true discloses him who is true; whatever is, is in him. "Everything was made in him, and without him was made nothing of that which was made" (John's Gospel, Prologue).

In his well-known love for creatures, Francis acts out this recognition of God's presence. He delights in the world of creation, and simply the touch of a creature can leave him enraptured. Francis continually exhorts every person and thing to "praise, bless and magnify the Creator." He treats them with deference and reverence, reminding his followers to be subject to every creature out of love for God. He calls every creature "brother" or "sister," and shows toward them, not simply curiosity or interest, but a tender affection.

Here is the full expression of God's identity: complete bowing over to offer the innermost reality of God as a gift. God's complete generosity is revealed in the Incarnation—nothing is held back, nothing is "property" to God, all is given away, God's true identity is communicated as poverty, holding on to nothing.

The religious world that humans developed cannot contain this mystery: God does not come as an angel or as a burst of light, not even as an idea or a vision—God comes as a baby. And the Word, incarnate, comes to a place and to people marked by poverty because these are most fitting to express the mystery—the surprising revelation of who God really is.

These theological reflections were not systematized by Francis, yet they help us to understand the importance of certain gestures and phrases of his. The feast of Christmas recalls that great humility and self-giving of God. Francis celebrates the feast dramatically, composing a living scene of animals and people in a cave at Greccio—recreating in his gesture the mystery of God's poor love.

Jesus shows in his life this identity of God in his choices, his words, his friends, his enemies, his gestures and signs. In the suffering he endures, and most fully in his Passion, Jesus reveals the unexpected identity of a God bowing over to give away all.

Even as he prepares to leave his friends, at table with them, Jesus continues to reveal this identity, so hard for them to accept. According to John's Gospel, he removes his outer garments, binds himself with a towel and bows over to wash their feet. Here is the true image of God. In the Synoptics, he takes the work of peasants' hands and gives away his own life as a cup of wine and a piece of bread.

These gestures are anticipations of the great giving away, the bowing over of death. Stripped of everything, pouring out his own lifeblood, water and blood flowing from his opened side, breathing forth his spirit, completely broken and emptied, suffering physical agony and spiritual desolation, Jesus at the moment of his death gives away God's own life.

Francis speaks of the "crucified poor, man," Christ, and knows that his death is the great act of God's loving graciousness. And in the Eucharist Francis recognizes the continuing gift—the Lord Jesus Christ gives himself fully as bread and wine. This divine life is given, eternally and irrevocably, for creatures.

The Trinitarian life of God, fully revealed and fully given away, shines with glorious joy in the Resurrection of Jesus, the glorification of Christ who becomes the first of creatures to be born into God. God's generosity now has opened the arms of the Trinity to every creature. Their full destiny is revealed—not only were they conformed to the Word in their origins, they are to be transformed in the Word as their fulfillment. All that God has given away begins its return to that personal and generous communion, glorified and transformed.

God's self-giving is a gift, freely given. The very life of God is a continual giving of self in the Trinity. The divine gift of life and communion is poured out through the Word. The Word, born as a creature, a person, is the full gift of God's own self.

In the life of Jesus, in his death, and his being raised up, the creation can finally, fully return to God as a gift, the gift of the Word. This circle of giving, in which Creator and creatures give all and receive all, rests on a single premise: that one does not hold back what has been given. When this happens, the gracious circle is broken, the exchange of gifts is interrupted, the whole creation risks losing its meaning and its very life.

In Franciscan terminology, this is a definition of sin—the sin described in Genesis, and the sin that follows: refusing to give away the gifts one has received.

For some Christian authors, the primary sin of Adam and Eve was pride, for others, it was disobedience. For Franciscans, it was the will to possess.

Reading the Genesis story in this light, we see the man and the woman are made "in the image and likeness of God." They receive all from God as a gift, and they give away all to God as praise and loving thanks. The serpent comes and proposes to offer them something, the fruit "that will make them like God." The offer is ludicrous: they are already like God. (The Father of Lies is at work with a trick as old as civilization—selling you what is already yours). The difference, of course, is that this time it will not be given as a gift; it will be taken, grasped, held onto.

And in this moment, the circle of the gift is broken. Harmony in creation fails. The image of God is obscured.

We begin to see here the reason for the preeminence of poverty and gratitude in Francis' vision. They are the two faces of this holy exchange of gifts: gratitude acknowledges that everything has been given to us, and poverty gives it all away.

This rapid survey of a Franciscan theological insight helps us to interpret words, gestures, and choices that Francis makes.

Francis marks the beginning of his new life with the sign of meeting the leper. Those suffering from leprosy in the thirteenth century lived a radical poverty. They were "dead" with funeral services celebrated over their still-living bodies. Their property was confiscated; their family ties, friendship and social relations were broken. They lived by the gifts of others.

"The Lord led me among them"—Francis attributes this leading to the Lord. "What was bitter to me became sweet." Francis finds among the lepers a quality, "sweetness," which he usually attributes to God's presence.

And he wishes to stay among them, to be with "persons looked down upon, among the poor, the weak, the sick and the lepers, and those begging on the side of the road." Among these, the persons looked down upon, Francis wishes to live. They are like Jesus "who was poor, and a guest, and lived by begging, himself and holy Mary the blessed virgin, his mother."

In the poor, Francis sees the image of Christ, the Image of God. The Lord Jesus Christ is poor in his birth, poor in his life, and poor in his death. And he wants to be in the world as one "looked down upon, needy and poor."

Francis embraces the leper, and with that gesture embraces the "holy Lady Poverty," and her sister, "holy humility." He does this out of a profound intuition that, through giving away everything, he will share in a truly divine activity; he will be accepting his true identity as made in the image of the poor God. "God created and formed you to the image of his beloved Son according to the body," Francis said, "all spiritual and bodily things and ourselves were made to your image and likeness."

With his discovery of God's poverty, Francis knows his own identity as made in God's image and recognizes his connection with all creatures—like him, they are images.

The Theology of Image

To speak of images and their place in Franciscan devotion we may begin quite simply, with a mirror. This could be a plain, square, modern mirror with an even and exact reflection. Or it could be the slightly corroded and uneven reflection of an antique Venetian mirror. We may even think of the surface of an ordinary mud puddle on a clear, windless day. It, too, is a kind of mirror.

Think perhaps of this poetic image given us by T.S. Eliot. While riding in a train through the English countryside one evening at sunset, he looks through the window of his carriage onto the beauty of rolling hills lit by the sun's warm, reddish glow. As darkness falls, the lights in the carriage illuminate more strongly the interior, and in the window Eliot sees now his own face in the place of the darkened countryside. The transparent glass changes to a reflecting surface, a mirror.

With these examples I am trying to approach, from our everyday experience, the theology of image, perhaps the most fundamental component of the Franciscan understanding of God, Christ, the human person, and the world. The Second Letter to the Corinthians (3:18) speaks of mirrors and images and for this reason, has been a favorite text of Franciscan spiritual writers for centuries. As Paul writes, "We all reflect as in a mirror the splendor of the Lord; thus we are transfigured into his likeness, from splendor to splendor, such is the influence of the Lord who is Spirit."

The image of the mirror that Paul uses is only one kind of image, the photograph is another. Since Franciscans have always preferred the concrete to the abstract, the specific to the universal, let me mention a single photograph, one from my adopted home, California. The photographer, Ansel Adams, died in 1984; the photograph he took he later named "Moon and Halfdome." In many ways this is a very ordinary picture. The moon rises over the great granite cliff called Halfdome, located in Yosemite National Park.

The photograph records exactly what the lens of the camera projected onto the chemicals of the photographic plate: a big, dark mass and a light, round sphere. Yet I can look at that photograph with a sense of wonder and delight, realizing that Adams aimed the lens in such a way as to balance the mass of rock with the brilliance of the full moon. As I look more closely at the picture I am puzzled by the photograph itself. I can see the rocky cliff, and I know that it really exists in the way the photograph shows it. But it also shows the moon, which I can see only from thousands of miles away, on the same paper surface with the cliff. Beyond the moon, it shows darkness, unbounded space. This darkness, in fact, makes up almost half of the photograph. The apparently infinite expanse of solar systems, galaxies, and emptiness sits in front of me, contained in an image that measures eight by fourteen inches. Infinity here fills a very small space. The paradox we observe in Adams' photography of cliff and moon puzzles us into admiration.

In a similar way, the mystery of the Incarnation has puzzled Franciscans into admiration.

Such a text as Colossians 1:15 has served as a source for profound meditation on that puzzle of who is Jesus: "He is the image of the invisible God; his is the primacy over all created things. In him everything in heaven and on earth was created...

The whole universe has been created through him and for him."

The great paradox here consists, not in an infinity of space captured within the bounds of a photograph, but in the supreme power and glory of God contained in a human person, Jesus of Nazareth, a poor and suffering man.

Since Franciscan theology is unavoidably autobiographical, please allow me to add an image that is uniquely mine. On June 22, 1983, I was sitting in an Italian train travelling between Turin and Aosta, toward the Alps along the Italian- French border. As the slow local train passed the ancient town of Ivrea, rain began to fall very gently. From my window I noticed alongside the tracks a puddle of dirty water. A few drops of rain made its surface uneven, and it reflected only haphazardly what was above it. But even that uneven reflection showed me part of a dark, powerful storm cloud looming overhead, out of my line of vision; then, in a flash of light, I glimpsed a single, powerful ray of sunlight burning the edge of that cloud with an almost blinding brightness. For a moment glory and menace, brilliance and gloom, the height of sun and clouds were encompassed in that dirty, rainspotted face.

That mud puddle has become for me an icon of Franciscan devotion to the mystery of the Incarnation, the discovery of the mystery of God's unspeakable transcendence in a few cubic feet of human flesh. This discovery has led Franciscan mystics and scholars to develop a theological reflection on Christ's centrality and primacy, a reflection that has grown from an experience of Christ in creation, especially the experience of Francis himself.

Spirituality of Christ as Center

Wherever one turns in Franciscan spirituality, one finds Christ. He functions as the center of devotion, of ministry, of life together, of authority, of charity. It is a truism to say that such a spirituality is Christocentric. The word, so technical in appearance, in fact breathes and moves beneath every authentically Franciscan text and life.

Christ becomes the answer to the philosophical question, "Why is there something and not nothing?" The answer is, "Because of Christ." From the atom to the universe, and including every level and phase of life and love within that compass, the radiating life and presence of Christ hold all things together as he vivifies and completes them.

While Christ must always be central to the faith of any Christian, there is a way in which we can speak of a special insistence on that centrality in the Franciscan tradition. We can speak of a "radical Christocentrism" which willingly sees Christ within human psychology, social life, mathematics and physics, music and drama. Wherever something or someone is, there is Christ. He is the inescapable, though often unrecognized, meaning behind all things.

Francis

The late Franciscan theologian, Fr. Eric Doyle, has written in this way about the importance of Christocentrism:

> If there is one word which does complete justice to Franciscan theology and spirituality it is "Christocentric," and they have this as their distinguishing feature, because the faith and holiness of St. Francis were totally centered on Christ. In Jesus Christ the revelation is made to us of what the world, as a whole and in all its parts, means to God.[1]

---

1   "St. Francis of Assisi and the Christocentric Character of Franciscan Life and Doctrine," in Damian McElrath, ed., *Franciscan Christology* (St.Bonaventure, NY: Franciscan Institute Publications, 1980), p.2.

The doctrine of Christ as center can already be found in Francis' own writings and has been developed by outstanding theologians, especially by Alexander of Hales and his student, Bonaventure. Later it takes on even greater importance in the teaching of John Duns Scotus.

Francis contributes to the tradition with his own insight about the central role of Christ in the *Rule* of 1221 where he writes: "All things spiritual and corporal were created through the Son." In a long meditation on these few, simple words, Doyle remarks:

> ...his devout love of the humanity of Jesus Christ brought him to understand that everything in heaven and on earth has been reconciled with God through Christ (Letter to a General Chapter). Francis reminds us all to realize the dignity God has bestowed on us: our body he formed and created in the image of his Son, our soul he made in his own likeness (Admonition V). This reflection is one of the most profound and far-reaching in the writings of St. Francis. For it seems clear that he is asserting in it that the first Adam was created after the image of the second Adam, Jesus Christ. The body of the Incarnate Word, Jesus of Nazareth, was the blueprint for the bodies of the first human beings. A little after the time of St. Francis, the learned doctor of the Order, Friar Alexander of Hales, explained that the image of God in whose likeness mankind was created, was the Saviour, who is the firstborn of all creatures... For all their simplicity and clarity, these sentences of Francis just quoted, have a rich theological content. Contained in embryo is the Christocentric vision of the Franciscan school and even the doctrine of Christ's absolute primacy as formulated and expounded by John Duns

Scotus.[2]

Bonaventure

Francis' deep appreciation of the centrality of Christ within the work of creation found its most eloquent theological expression in the works of Bonaventure. Zachary Hayes has explained that, in the growth of Bonaventure's theology, Christ becomes more and more the central concern. In Hayes' words, "The core of the Christological mystery is the fact that in Jesus the center of all reality has become incarnate and has been made historically visible."[3]

Bonaventure's meditation on the theme of the image uses the notion of the "exemplar." We might say that the exemplar is the person standing in front of the mirror, and the reflection in the mirror is an image of the exemplar. As Bonaventure conceived it, using the beautiful metaphor of the artist at work: God is the exemplar of all things (the artist's interior concept), the humanity of Jesus is the expression of the exemplar (the artwork created by the artist), all creation is formed in Christ (artworks modeled on the original work). Bonaventure himself explains it in this way:

> One [exemplar] is interior, in the mind of the artist, as the cause according to which the artist produces his works. The other is exterior; it is that to which one who is ignorant of art looks and by which he is directed in a certain way, just as mechanical artists have certain forms external to themselves according to which they direct their works, as is clear in the case of shoemakers.[4]

2   *Ibid.*, p. 7.

3   "The Life and Christological Thought of St. Bonaventure," in McElrath, p. 63.

4   *Ibid.*, p. 79.

This signified that Christ is the blueprint, the form, or the inspiring image that God uses as a model in molding every part of creation. The human person in a special way reveals that creative model. This theological understanding of Christ as image can be read as an extended meditation on a brief statement from Francis found in his Fifth Admonition: "Consider... how excellent the Lord made you, for he created and formed you to the image of his beloved son according to the body and to his own likeness according to the spirit."[5]

That brief text may be read as the inspiration for many later developments in Franciscan theological tradition, containing in germ the essential components of later reflections on anthropology, Christology, and the theology of image.

A Franciscan named John Duns Scotus meditated earnestly on Bonaventure's figure of Christ as the center of all things. Before his untimely death in 1308 at the age of forty-two, John had developed his own expression of Christocentrism. Scotus built another level of the friars' intellectual tradition in his theological and philosophical works.

Scotus tried to resolve a difficulty he found in the works of many Christian theologians. To put it simply, the problem concerned this expression, "Christ came because Adam sinned." In Scotus' day and in ours, many would not find any difficulty with that phrase. Christ came in order to repair the harm done by the sin of our first parents. No doubt, even Scotus would admit, the phrase expresses something quite true. Yet he remained unsatisfied—that phrase could not explain the fullest or best reason for the Incarnation of the Word. Why not? In his own technical language,

---

5   Quoted in Allan Wolter, "John Duns Scotus on the Primacy and Personality of Christ," in McElrath, p. 141.

Scotus argued, "It is not likely that the highest good in the whole of creation is something that merely happened by chance, and happened only because of some lesser good."[6]

In our words, we might explain this in the following way. The Incarnation of the Word is the highest good, the supreme expression of God's love. By comparison with the infinity of love revealed in the Incarnation, Adam's sin and correcting its effects appear as a lesser good. (To use a metaphor, why build the Taj Mahal to cover a pothole?) The solution is not in proportion to the problem to be solved. Furthermore, the theory refuted by Scotus implies that the Incarnation was an accident of sorts, that it happened by chance. If Adam had not sinned, there would be no need for the Incarnation. (An echo of this thinking can be heard in the *Exultet* of the Easter Vigil: *O felix culpa*, "O happy fault! O necessary sin of Adam!")

Scotus proposed his own reasons for the coming of Christ in this way: "I say that the incarnation of Christ was not foreseen as occasioned by sin, but was immediately foreseen from all eternity by God as a good more proximate to the end."[7] This statement, in technical medieval language, may need some translation. The end here refers to God's purpose or goal for the whole of creation. That goal, according to Scotus, is the sharing of God's own life, one so fruitful that it constantly seeks expression. The ultimate goal must be sharing the life of the Trinity itself. Within the Trinity, the Second Person, the Son or Word, is the center, or middle member. The Son may be called the heart of or the way into the Trinity. As the self-diffusive love of the Trinity is expressed in the act of creation, the Son is the Image or Form for everything God creates.

6   *Ibid.*, pp. 150-1.

7   *Franciscan Christology.* p. 153.

Now, if God's ultimate goal for creation is participation in the divine life, the Incarnation of the Son is a "good" very close to the goal or, in Scotus' words, "more proximate to the end." Why? Because Christ becomes the bridge or the middle member, linking the creation, particularly humanity, to the inner life of God. Christ becomes the necessary gate or way into God's life, the ultimate goal intended for all creation.

Imitation and Love

This appreciation of the Incarnation underlies the Franciscan emphasis on repeating the actions of Jesus, the starting- point for devotional practices focused on the physical reconstruction of saving events, accessible to all, regardless of education or wealth. The origin of the Christmas creche, for example, shows Francis' insistence on reproducing in visible, tangible form the mystery of the Incarnation at Bethlehem, otherwise available only to a few privileged pilgrims to the East. Later Franciscan devotions, like that of the Way of the Cross in the Eighteenth Century, offered to the ordinary believer the opportunity to participate physically in a symbolic walk with Christ through the events of his passion and death, an opportunity otherwise restricted to those able to travel to Jerusalem.

The Franciscan way into the mysteries of the life of Christ does not move primarily through principles or ideals that can be abstracted from experience, but through learning by imitation, a reenacting of the life of Jesus in order to experience, from within, his reactions to children, lepers, the possessed, and the Pharisees.

The desire to be like Jesus has led Franciscans to emphasize the importance of imitation as a means of participation. One notices here an implicit trust in the value of giving a cup of cold water to the thirsty over abstracting a principle about the meaning of cold water in first-century Palestine. We could say that Franciscans have displayed a "sacramental consciousness," an awareness of the value of signs, gestures, actions as pedagogical tools in Christian life.

Following from the notion of imitation comes the supreme appreciation of the *form* of God's love for humanity. That love is a crucified love or, in personal terms, it is Crucified Love.

Two major forms of approach to God may be summarized under the rubrics of "God as Truth" and "God as Love." These receive differing emphases in different Christian spiritual traditions, and there are undoubtedly other effective rubrics for explaining the way in which we approach God. The Franciscan tradition has consistently given greater emphasis to the rubric of love, of affectivity and the will in treating of our life of journeying toward God. Ultimately, for these masters of the spiritual life, the will and the affections lead a person most surely toward the heart of God, revealed as the burning love of the Crucified.

While respecting knowledge as a vehicle bearing believers toward union, this tradition emphasizes a wisdom wider than knowledge, one which takes the place of the heart seriously. We are, in fact, not only rational animals but, even more deeply, feeling animals. While this should not be construed as an open door to sentimentality in religious growth (it has sometimes degenerated into that), this tradition has at its core a wonderfully full and rich appreciation of the human person as a whole being, one in which the powers of thinking and feeling are not opposed but rather in which feeling complements and fulfills the functions of thinking.

Franciscan saints, mystics, theologians, poets and artists have never tired of the theme of the crucifixion of Love as the beginning and goal of all authentic union with God. There is for them no escape from the wounds of the Savior; there is no escape from the definitive act of self-giving in Jesus' laying down his life for his friends.

In theological terms, Bonaventure tells us that in the journey of the soul into God the highest point of mystical union comes in embracing the Crucified. This is the way into the very life of God. There is no transcending or passing over the fact that the Risen Savior is risen from the Cross and bears in his glorified life the marks of human suffering and death. The story of the doubts of Thomas serves to underscore this truth for Franciscan authors.

The Word of God comes to us as a human being, Jesus of Nazareth. The Word also comes to us in the Scriptures of the Old and New Testaments, especially through the "Holy Gospel of our Lord Jesus Christ." The Word comes to us in a concrete, physical way in the form of bread and wine at the Eucharist. It is one and the same Word who comes to us in these different ways, the same one who came to Mary as her son.

This understanding will help us to grasp the interrelationship of three motifs in Franciscan devotion: devotion to the Scriptures, to the Eucharist, to Mary and the Church.

Mary is the dwelling place, the tabernacle of God's Word, which she treasures in her heart and offers to the world as her child. So Francis speaks of her in his "Salutation of the Virgin."[8]

So the Church serves as a bearer of the Word, after the example of the woman who gives the Word to the world. The Church, like Mary, is human, yet transformed by the gift of the Holy Spirit into the Spouse of the Spirit. She, the Church, is also tabernacle, dwelling-place of the Word. Therefore, Francis says

8   Armstrong-Brady, p. 149.

with irrefutable logic that Mary is "the virgin made Church."[9]

Francis commands his brothers that they should show great respect for words written on even tiny scraps of paper. The letters written there may contain the name of the Lord. The simple, humble piece of paper becomes iconic, a sign of the Word to Francis. Respect for words, and our use of words, derives from his consuming love for the one who is God's Word to us.

In a similar manner Francis' respect for churches parallels his respect for bits of paper or parchment. These buildings occupy an important place in Francis' biography as concrete, literally concrete, dwellings for the Word. Thus the friars are to show great respect for churches since these are places wherein the Word dwells sacramentally in the Eucharist. Hence Francis' prayer, "We adore You, Lord Jesus Christ, in all Your churches throughout the world, and we bless You, for through Your holy cross You have redeemed the world."[10]

The Franciscan Way of Life and Its Purpose

It is all very well to have a theology, to develop a spirituality, and to have an impact on popular devotional life. But a spiritual tradition must do other things in order to survive and flourish within the Church. It must have a form of life, some system of relationships, structures and programs that help to translate the vision into lived experience, and to turn the lived experience constantly toward its founding vision.

The Franciscan "form" may be called the *vita evangelica*, the evangelical life, the Gospel life. That in itself would not seem to distinguish it from the ordinary life of dedication lived by any

---

9   *Ibid.*

10   *Ibid.* p. 154.

committed Christian. However, the reader may find, on closer analysis, that the specific meaning and interpretation of that term contains much that is distinctive.

First of all, Franciscans intend to live the whole Gospel. Again, this may not seem surprising. But in fact most traditions within the Church claim to live one facet, or a couple of important dimensions of the Gospel. For example, one group may intend to imitate the hidden life of Jesus, while another models itself on Jesus the preacher during his public ministry. A third may seek to model itself on the suffering of the Lord, and a fourth on the glory of Christ's resurrection.

Franciscans have claimed from the very beginning that they wished to live every part of the Gospel, the "full Gospel." This desire to include all the many parts of the Gospel within its life has led the Franciscan family, in its many branches, to live with paradox, even seeming contradiction. The following pages will sketch some important features of the Franciscan way of life, showing how it includes many different parts of the "full Gospel."

The Hermitage and the Workplace

Because they wished to live all the Gospel, the new form of life Franciscans inaugurated fit neither the category of the contemplative nor the active life as these were being defined. They were classified as being of "mixed life," that is, both contemplative and active. This characteristic can help us to understand how the Franciscan family can include full-time contemplatives and missionaries, heads of families and hermits within its wide embrace. They all form a part of the whole, and the Gospel demands that wholeness.

Clare serves as a reminder that the Franciscan movement at its origins has no need to struggle with the issue of the importance and centrality of the contemplative life, but rather with the question of preaching and its place within a life dedicated to the spirit of "prayer and holy devotion."

In the *Major Life* of Francis by Bonaventure, Francis asks two people to help him discern the shape of his life. The two people are Sylvester, one of the brothers, and Clare. His question was this: Could he best serve God by living in a hermitage or by preaching? Clare and Sylvester prayed about this matter, and both replied that he should continue preaching.

The question, as Bonaventure presents it, probably concerned others besides Francis. Clare lived as a "contemplative" (to use our modern categories); Sylvester, a priest, is known to us chiefly as a hermit, another contemplative. The question is directed to these two trusted advisors, and their answer is that Francis continue the "active" life of preaching.

Yet the terms "active" and "contemplative" are rather misleading when speaking of the early Franciscans. Neither Francis nor Clare use the word "contemplative." They do speak of "contemplation" in various ways, Clare more often than Francis, but it refers generally to "looking at" or "beholding."

Both Francis and Clare speak of the "spirit of prayer" as a guiding principle in the life of their brothers and sisters. And both expect that work will be an essential part of their lives.

The Brothers and Sisters of Penance, those who live in their own homes, have families and occupations in society, are called to a contemplative life of prayer in the circumstances of their lives.

Clare and her sisters give a special witness to the contemplative dimension of the Franciscan vocation. In solitude and communion as sisters, the Poor Sisters express this gift in complete poverty, mutual love, liturgical prayer, attentive listening to the Word of

God, and in work.

This life is a form of preaching. Clare asks her sisters to live this evangelical life "in the sight of all" so that by their example people may be brought to Christ, to be "a mirror and example for all living in the world."

Francis writes a *Rule* especially for those brothers who live in hermitages, and in his own life witnesses to the importance of the contemplative foundation of his life of conversion. His biographers picture Francis spending as much as seven months a year living in the silence and solitude of the many early Franciscan hermitages. In these places (Greccio, Fonte Colombo, and La Verna among others) three or four brothers lead a contemplative life, alternating roles of "mothers" and "sons."

This easy exchange of roles which we would call active and contemplative shows the difficulty of characterizing Francis' "form of life" as being *either* contemplative *or* active. It is quite simply, fully both.

Francis himself frequently lived in these solitary places, frequently celebrating a "Lent" of fasting and prayer. His biographers indicate that he observed as many as five "Lents." These included the Lent of the Incarnation from the Feast of All Saints in early November until Christmas, and another period from the feast of the Epiphany in January to the beginning of what we usually call Lent, the Great Lent of the Redemption for forty days before Easter. From the feast of Saints Peter and Paul in late June until the feast of the Assumption in mid-August he observed another period of solitude and prayer. From the Assumption until late September he observed a Lent that ended with the feast of Saint Michael the Archangel. We do not know whether Francis observed all of these Lents every year. If he did, more than half the year was dedicated to contemplative solitude: early November through March or April (depending on the date of Easter), and late June through September.

Other brothers imitated this practice to a greater or lesser degree—they were obliged only to observe the "Great Lent" before Easter and the "Lent" preceding Christmas. We can suppose that some would spend this time in the hermitages, alternating that form of life with the more "active" life of the suburban places and preaching journeys. Some brothers seem to have stayed at the hermitages year round. Whatever the time individual brothers may have spent in the hermitage, it was an important component of the life of the early fraternity of Lesser Brothers.

Franciscans and the University

The life which is both active and contemplative is also one in which study has played a role from a very early time. In his *Rule* of 1223, Francis refers to work when he says the brothers should work in such a way as not to "extinguish the Spirit of holy prayer and devotion, to which all other things of our earthly existence must contribute."[11] If the "Letter to Anthony" is, as some think, an authentic work of Francis, it echoes those same sentiments in regard to study, specifically theological study.[12]

During Francis' life the friars had already arrived at the leading intellectual centers of their day: Paris, Oxford, Cambridge, Bologna. A geography of early Franciscan settlements in England shows strikingly how the friars sought out the civic center (London), the ecclesiatical center (Canterbury), and the cultural center (Oxford) of thirteenth-century England.

---

11   Armstrong-Brady, p. 140.

12   *Ibid.,* p. 49.

In France, the early settlement at Paris began as a loan of property from the canons of the church of Saint-Germain-des-Prés. Shortly after, the friars received property along the Seine, the site of what would later be known as *le Grand Couvent*. It was situated in what is now known as the Latin Quarter, the University district.

Franciscans brought something distinctive to the new university system of Europe. Their profound reflection on the mystery of the Incarnation and their firm belief in the person as image of God helped to lay the foundations for a "Franciscan theology."

The first great name associated with this movement was a contemporary of Francis, Anthony, known to us today as St. Anthony of Padua. The first "professor" of the new Order, Anthony entered the friars with a degree already completed. Formerly an Augustinian canon in Portugal, he had already been a teacher of Scriptural studies before entering the Order.

Shortly afterward another scholar entered the Order: his name was Master Alexander of Hales, an Englishman who already held a "tenured" position at Paris and brought with him to the Franciscan house the power to grant degrees. With his colleague, the Frenchman Jean de la Rochelle, Alexander helped to form the young Bonaventure, then a student, later to be the premier theologian of the Franciscan School.

Later generations saw the important contributions of Franciscans to the theological and cultural world. Cardinal Ximenes de Cisneros, a friar, and regent of Spain, prepared his famous *Biblia Complutensis* or Polyglot Bible, published in 1517 at the University of Alcalá, founded by him. The Bible was translated into French by another friar, Guillaume Le Menan, about 1585, on orders from Louis XI.

Among scholar-mystics there were also notable figures from the family of St. Francis. In the great constellation of Rheno-Flemish authors (Ruysbroeck, Tauler, Eckhart), there was also a notable Franciscan: Henry de Herp, or Harphius (d. 1477). Guardian of the friary at Malines, he was a famous preacher and spiritual writer, an important influence over the next two centuries, both inside and outside Brabant, notably in sixteenth-century Spain. His *Mirror of Perfection* and the *Mystical Theology* show a personal synthesis of Franciscan doctrine.

Rabelais, himself a Franciscan, and his superior at the friary of Fontenay kept up a correspondence with humanists of their day. Jean Vitrier, guardian of the friars at Saint-Omer, a remarkable professor, is known to us through the admirable portrait of him left by Erasmus in his letter to Josse Jonas. Vitrier said, not without reference perhaps to currents of reform sweeping the Franciscan world, "It would be a sin to insist on exaggerated fasts and thus, over a question of nourishment and penance, to compromise sacred studies."[13]

The great humanist Erasmus even had comments to make about the state of the Franciscan Order at the dawn of humanism:

> St. Francis has become great before God and men, because of virtue, not scandal. One does not imitate him by having bare feet, a cord of wool, and a robe of homespun. I have attacked abuses and prejudice wherever I found them, but have never attacked any Order. I have only criticized the exaggerations of certain monks who have more respect for the Rule of St. Francis

---

13   Quoted in Vorreux, p. 304.

than for the Gospel.[14]

Currents of reform within the Lesser Brothers encountered determined and sometimes picturesque opposition from the brethren in the intellectual centers of the Order. Olivier Maillard, serving a third term as Vicar General of the Ultramontane Observants, attempted in 1502 to bring reform to the Great Friary of Paris (*le Grand Couvent*) by assigning fifty friars belonging to the reform movement to the Paris community. His purpose was to make this group the kernel of a reconversion in that large community where nearly three hundred fifty young friars were studying at the time. The community refused to admit the newcomers. Georges d'Amboise, cardinal legate, ordered two bishops to make a solemn visit to impose the reform on the house. The friars, hearing of the impending visit, exposed the Blessed Sacrament on the altar and began singing the Office. As the bishops entered, the choir intoned: *Adjuva nos, Deus, salutaris noster!* And each time the bishops tried to speak, the friars began a new psalm. After four hours of this "liturgical obstructionism" the bishops retreated. The next day, however, the bishops returned, this time with a king's officer and one hundred trained archers. "The sight of the archers inspired prudence," so the bishops were able to announce the reforms. But one does not catch so many assembled doctors napping.

> They defended their argument by showing titles, rules, authorities, reasons and examples, and by having carried into their chapter the Decretals and Clementines, dispensations and privileges, and all the laws they could use to help them.[15]

---

14   Quoted in Vorreux, p. 306.

15   Vorreux, p. 306.

They won: a commission was named to study the modalities of the reform proposed, and that was the end of the reform.

Franciscan authors contributed much to the "Golden Age" of Spanish mysticism of the sixteenth century. Teresa of Avila took Franciscan authors as guides and teachers, including Alonso de Madrid, with his *Arte para servir a Dios*; Francisco de Osuna, author of *The Third Spiritual Alphabet*; Bernardine of Laredo, laybrother, physician, and author of *The Ascent of Mount Sion*; and Peter of Alcantara.

Among their first great masters, the Capuchins list Benoit de Canfield (William Fitch, d.1610), a converted English Puritan who received exceptional mystical graces. His *Rule of Perfection* shows that all holiness returns to doing God's will and allowing God to direct one's actions.

A pioneer of modern critical historical research in this era was Luke Wadding (1588-1657). An Irishman who studied at the College of Lisbon and the University of Coimbra, he later entered the Order and edited the writings of St. Francis in 1623. In 1625 he founded St. Isidore's College in Rome, and in 1639 published the twelve in-folio volumes of the *Opera omnia* of Scotus.

Lawrence of Brindisi, the great Capuchin author, excelled as an exegete, theologian, and widely respected patristic scholar. The Conventual, Cardinal Brancati, was an eminent Scotist whose works reflected his expertise on the Franciscan themes of the Incarnation and kingship of Christ.

Running like a thread through their intellectual activities is the hint that Franciscans generally looked upon themselves as preachers of one sort or another, their task to proclaim the Good News of Christ in manifold ways. Francis had given the example of imitating the Lord in this, sending his own followers out two by two into the towns and villages to proclaim the Kingdom of God. His followers continued in that practice, adapting it to new circumstances over the years. That dimension of the Franciscan life now deserves our attention.

Franciscan Mission

A challenge to be, for today's world, what great pioneers were in the past led a German Jesuit to make the following observation a half century ago:

> The principle that led, through Benedict to Dominic and on to Ignatius, to the organization of more recent religious congregations seems to be nearing the term of its inner possibilities of development. This does not mean to say, of course, that it will ever be superfluous or replaceable. But a fundamentally new guide-line, sought for by so many, and experimented in new foundations, especially today, can probably be found on a quite different tack, namely that of the primitive Franciscan ideal: unhampered vivaciousness in a free community of love, that expresses itself spontaneously without being forced into the mold of prescriptions and ordinances, developing personalities according to their own essential nature, both vital and original, obeying their own inmost law of discipline and self-command. If God should grace His Church one day with the Order of the future, for which so many of the best are yearning today, then it will probably bear the imprint of St. Francis' inspiration.[16]

Those words, written more than fifty years ago, could make

---

16   Peter Lippert, SJ, in *Stimmen der Zeit*, 1927, quoted in *Charism* 1:10.

today's Franciscans blush, in part from pride but also from embarrassment. The Church expects much from the followers of the Little Poor Man of Assisi, and the task of living out his ideal can seem at times almost impossible: to realize expectations of the very highest order.

In no other area is the living out of that ideal more challenging today than in the area of "mission." In many ways the characteristic Franciscan approach to mission organizes the understanding of Franciscan life. The Franciscan mission is a life, the "evangelical life," expressed in various ways in the *Rules* and *Constitutions* of different members of the Family.

The friars' *Rule* of 1223 begins with this expression: "The Rule and life of the lesser brothers is this, *to observe the Holy Gospel* of our Lord Jesus Christ." St. Clare, in her *Rule* for the Poor Ladies, remarks on the profound unity of vision she and her sisters shared with Francis:

(Francis) noticed that we did not fear poverty, labor, sorrow, humiliation and contempt from the world... (He wrote) "you have made yourselves, under divine inspiration, daughters and maids of the most sublime, the mightiest king, the heavenly Father, and have made yourselves the spouses of the Holy Spirit by choosing a *life according to the Holy Gospel...*"[17]

The *Rule* of the Franciscan Third Order Religious begins with the same emphasis:

The form of life of the brothers and sisters of the Third Order Regular of St. Francis is this: *to observe the Holy Gospel* of our

---

17   Quoted in *Charism* 5:8 Cf. Armstrong-Brady, p. 218.

Lord Jesus Christ.[18]

Franciscans understand their form of life as already being a mission. And this affects the way they understand particular activities as an expression of their basic mission of "living according to the Gospel." As the Friars Minor expressed it in 1972:

> The essential mission of our fraternity, its vocation to the Church and to the world, consists in the lived reality of our life commitment... it is in our way of life that we bear witness.[19]

For Franciscans, mission is incarnated in personal living. *The great mission is Jesus himself*: Jesus reveals to humanity who God is and this in two ways: by words (saying who God is); and by actions (showing who God is). This mission originates in God's love, so great as to send the only-begotten Son (Jn 3:16). Jesus' mission reveals in different ways who God is, as Francis says: he "has condescended to pray to the Father and to make his Name known to us."[20]

This revelation of who God is, Jesus' mission, already finds expression in the creation. The good world, with the human person at its center, shows people who God is. The harmony of creation, broken by sin, is restored in Jesus, the enfleshed Word.

The movement of the Franciscan mission begins here, as Francis sends his followers into the whole world with the words:

---

18   See Martino Conti, *L'identità francescana del Fratelli e delle Sorelle del Terzo Ordine Regolare di San Francesco: Commento alla nuova Regola* (Bologna): Movimento Francescano, 1986), p. 23.

19   "The Vocation of the Order Today," n. 31, from the Chapter of Madrid, 1972, in *Charism* 2:16.

20   *Charism* 3:4. Cf. Armstrong-Brady, p. 129.

(That) by word and deed you might bear witness to His message and convince everyone that there is no other Almighty God besides Him.[21]

And this message of the one God is that of Jesus' prayer, union in love, a message quoted by Francis in the early *Rule*: "that all the world might recognize that you have loved them as You have loved me, that the love with which You have loved me might be in them and I in them."[22]

Mission, in Francis' view, does not mean merely speaking a message, nor even undertaking certain activities. Mission is the revelation of God through living among others in this good world. Living according to the Gospel is always "missionary," it reveals who God is.

A part of this mission of "living according to the Holy Gospel" is mutual care and love. "If a mother loves and nourishes her child according to the flesh," Francis writes, "how much more should the brothers love and care for one another."[23] The members of the fraternity reveal God to each other through brotherly affection.

Particular characteristics of God's love, revealed in Jesus, should move the brothers to be "peaceable, kind, gentle and humble,"[24] as Jesus was meek and humble of heart.[25]

Their love should also bear suffering after the pattern of

---

21 *Charism* 3:8. Cf. Armstrong-Brady, p. 56.

22 *Charism* 3:6. From Jn. 17:23, 26. Cf Armstrong-Brady, p. 130.

23 Cf. Armstrong-Brady, p. 141.

24 *Charism* 3:9. Cf. Armstrong-Brady, p. 139.

25 Mt. 11:29.

Jesus who offered himself freely to those who crucified him.[26] Making themselves "subject to every creature," they should avoid "quarrelling and entering into disputes" with those who oppose them.[27]

Surprising as it may seem, this peaceful and patient love serves as Francis' first "method" for proclaiming the Gospel in the world of Islam. Speaking about the brothers whom God inspires to "go among Saracens and other unbelievers," Francis says they may announce the Good News in this way: "they should begin neither quarrels nor dissensions, but should be subject to every human creature for God's sake, and acknowledge that they are Christians."[28]

Considering that these words were written at the time of the Fifth Crusade, they may strike us as particularly significant in their emphasis on the peacefulness and humility which Christians should show among their Muslim neighbors.

At certain times this mission may involve a simple exhortation to Christian faith, "another way" to announce the Good News, and one that God may inspire at different times. As Francis writes:

> Another way is to proclaim the word of God openly, when they see it is God's will, calling on their hearers to believe in God Almighty, Father, Son and Holy Spirit, the Creator of all, and in the Son, the Redeemer and Savior, that they may be baptized and become Christians.[29]

---

26   Armstrong-Brady, p. 121.

27   *Charism* 3:9. Cf. Armstrong-Brady, p. 121.

28   *Ibid.*

29   *Charism* 4:8. Cf. Armstrong-Brady, pp. 121-122.

A Global Mission

From its beginnings in Francis' mission among Muslims of North Africa, the Franciscan project of proclaiming the Good News spread to embrace six continents.[30]

In the Far East, Odoric of Pordenone followed the route of the Franciscan pioneers, John of Piancarpino and John of Montecorvino. In 1314 he left Venice by ship, crossed into Persia from Kurdestan, and reached the Indian Ocean. After following the coast of Malabar and a long detour among the islands of Indonesia, he arrived in China where he found many Franciscan friaries and their Christian populations, notably those in the Italian colony at Beijing and the friary at Zayton (Quanzhou) facing Taiwan, which already offered hospitality to European merchants passing through. Odoric settled in Tibet and returned to Europe only to die in 1331.

Activity in the Near East continued during the same century. On July 11, 1309, the Friars of the Cord received permission to reside at the Holy Places (Mt. Sion, the Holy Sepulcher, Bethlehem) in a document signed by Sultan Baibars II. This document recognizing the right of Franciscans to reside at those places is still in effect. This Province, the Sacred Custody of the Holy Land, has been the special care of the Order since Francis himself went there to walk in Christ's steps. Pope Gregory IX officially designated Franciscans as "Guardians of the Holy Land" in 1230.

The evangelizing activity of the Franciscans reached Japan[31] where the persecution in Nagasaki of 1597 claimed numerous victims among the Franciscans, both friars and lay penitents. The Philippines, one of the most flourishing missions, could boast

---

30   See Iriarte, Part One, Chap. 12, "Missions to Non-Catholic Peoples," pp. 133-148.

31   *Ibid.*, Part Two, Chap. 10, "The Missions," pp. 303-346.

colleges and hospitals for victims of leprosy. India rivalled the Philippine mission. The first archbishop of Goa, the Franciscan Juan de Albuquerque, was viceroy of the East Indies and aided St. Francis Xavier in Goa.

On the arrival of Europeans in the Americas, Franciscans were the first called to serve as missionaries in the "New" World.[32] Two Spanish friars accompanied Columbus on his second voyage in 1493. The first Franciscan province was established on Española in 1505, and soon friars arrived in modern-day Santo Domingo, Colombia, Venezuela, and Mexico. Within twenty five years they had settled in Peru, Nicaragua, and Panama. Foundations soon sprang up in Bolivia, Chile, and Equador.

In the early 1600s, French Recollect friars came to Canada. By mid-century Portuguese Franciscans had settled in Brazil. In the English American colonies, a few Franciscans came to work after 1673.

The Province of Santa Elena of Florida, headquartered in Havana, Cuba, in 1612, sent friars throughout what is now the southeastern United States, establishing missions in Florida and Georgia. The first missions in Texas were founded by friars from Mexico in 1690, and by the middle of the next century they had settled in Arizona. In the 1770s, under the leadership of fray (Blessed) Junipero Serra, Franciscans came to California. The chain of California Missions along the Pacific coast remains the best-known reminder of the long history of the Franciscans in the

---

32   Information in this section is taken from Lino Gómez Canedo OFM, "Franciscans in the Americas: A Comprehensive View," pp. 5-45, in Francisco Morales OFM, ed., *Franciscan Presence in the Americas: Essays on the Activities of the Franciscan Friars in The Americas*, 1492-1900 (Potomac, MD: Academy of American Franciscan History, 1983). See also John Leddy Phelan, *The Millennial Kingdom of the Franciscans in the New World*, second edition, revised (Berkeley and Los Angeles: University of California Press, 1970).

territory of the United States today.

From Past to Present

These accomplishments are those of the past. Discoverers and explorers, sometimes adventurers, Franciscans brought the Gospel to many areas of the world in times that seem to us very distant. These pages are those of a family history, and the glimpses we see of scholars and mystics, contemplatives and missionaries remind us that they have given a heritage to Franciscans today.

If we listen to this history as a kind of Franciscan symphony, we can pick out some recurring themes, sometimes played in minor key, at other time transposed to a single major chord, all accompanied by variations on the theme.

These themes certainly include that of poverty, a perpetual challenge to the family. Another theme is that of the contemplative dimension of our life and the ways this is integrated with many different kinds of work, from the university classroom to the missionary expedition.

A theme running through moments of new foundations is that of participation, for women and men, clerics, religious and laity. Sometimes more, sometimes less, Franciscans have lived up to their ideal of being a family, brothers and sisters to each other.

Now it is time to speak about Franciscans today, and to speak of different corners of the world so thoroughly travelled by their brothers and sisters of the past.

6

Franciscans Today

History can become a divisive property, written by protagonists of painful divisions and revindicators of greater perfection. The great battles are recounted, old grievances are revived. One generation passes on to the next the stories, the memories of triumphs and wounds. It may only be a coincidence that in 1517 the Order of Francis' brothers divided into two mutually hostile branches, the Western Church divided into mutually hostile bodies, and in Sicily the Mafia began. Within ten years the Franciscans re-divided to form a third branch, the Church divided further, and the Mafia grew. And all these groups remain to this day.

But what is today's state of that family which is the subject of this book? And what are the relations among the various branches of that family today?

Vatican II

The Second Vatican Council asked religious families to re-examine their life and their testimony to Christ in the contemporary world. The Council called for a return to "the charism of the founder" and Franciscans responded energetically to this mandate. A fundamentally important task was that of knowing what the founder actually wrote and to understand better the charism he lived.

The task was not an easy one and remains difficult. The Franciscans of the 1960s were heirs to traditions of interpreting Francis begun in the late nineteenth century and carried forward in the first half of this century. The nineteenth century had "rediscovered" Francis through the eyes of the Romantic Movement and Protestant scholarship. Francis was the poet of nature; the prophet of world peace, the troubadour of courtly love, the rebel; a nonconformist conformed to a Roman ecclesiastical pattern by outside pressure, he was "the first Protestant," "a true socialist," and the medieval hero for modern times.

A figure as fascinating and contradictory as Francis of Assisi could hardly fail to provide ammunition to opposing camps in battles over social, religious and political differences. An opposing tendency pictured Francis as the father of Italian nationalism, in the words of the Fascist Mussolini: "the most saintly of Italians and the most Italian of saints." He was portrayed by some Catholic scholars as the model supporter of the Papacy, the entirely submissive and obedient son of the Roman Church, implacable opponent of heresy and schism. The little poor man, lover of Lady Poverty, was also the model merchant, the first great saint produced by the urban bourgeoisie.

The discussions on the interpretation of Francis had as their focus the so-called "biographies" of the saint—secondary sources written by others more or less reliable in their judgments of how Francis lived and what he said.

A major change in the focus of discussion was due to

increasing attention to the writings of Francis himself. New tools of textual interpretation used in both historical and scriptural studies allowed scholars to produce new and corrected versions of Francis' own writings. The great Franciscan scholar Kajetan Esser produced a critical edition of the writings in 1976 and this work has gradually borne fruit in the numerous contemporary studies of the "charism" of Francis himself.

A New Climate

The search for a better understanding of the Franciscan charism has borne fruit in other ways. In the climate of ecumenism encouraged by the Council, efforts toward Franciscan ecumenism assumed greater importance. The Ministers General of the Family (Conventuals, Minors, Capuchins, and Third Order Regular) began to meet regularly. The General Superiors of men's and women's congregations of Third Order religious expanded and intensified their common bonds. The Poor Clares strengthened their federations. The Secular Franciscans began to work on the revision of their *Rule,* those affiliated with various branches of the Friars Minor working together.

The study of our shared roots has led to common initiatives: a pilgrimage to Assisi and celebrations for the 750th anniversary of Francis' death in 1976 and the 800th anniversary of his birth in 1982.

The Franciscan women's movement has played an important role here, offering leadership to the Franciscan Federation of Brothers and Sisters in the United States, the Movimento Religiose Francescane (MO.RE.FRA) in Italy, and similar initiatives in other countries.

In 1985 a further, important step was taken with the establishment of the International Conference of the Brothers and Sisters of the Third Order Regular of St. Francis (I.F.C.). Approximately 365 Franciscan women's and 20 men's congregations belong to the new body, among whose purposes is the strengthening of efforts toward inter-Franciscan cooperation.

What does it mean to be a Franciscan today? It means a return to the "spirit of the founder" urgently requested by the Second Vatican Council. Since that appeal was made two decades ago, the many members of the Franciscan Family have set about rediscovering their identity.

The appeal made by the Council was welcome. A certain "homogenization" of life and ideals had made many communities within the Church resemble each other—in their activity, their form of life, their spirituality. The Council posed the question, "What do you offer that is unique, what role do you play that others do not fill?"

A period of long and sometimes painful self-examination led to a conviction: we need a fuller understanding of Francis, of Clare, of the beginning of the Brothers and Sisters of Penance.

An important step in this direction was taken with the publication of a new, critical text of Francis' writings and those of Clare. A renewed understanding of Francis *Rule* is reflected in the recently reformulated Constitutions of Capuchins, Conventuals and Friars Minor. The Secular Franciscan Order revised its *Rule*, confirmed by Pope Paul VI in 1978. The friars of the Third Order Regular, with brothers and sisters of the Third Order tradition for religious, elaborated a renewed, common *Rule*.

Poor Clare delegates have met to revise Constitutions whose approval will signal an important step in the renewal of the contemplative life in the tradition of Clare of Assisi.

A Sense of Family

The emphasis on differences between the various branches has begun to shift, and the term "Franciscan Family" is now often used. This term points to the common heritage shared by those who follow the example and inspiration of the Poverello, the little poor man of Assisi.

Though still far from perfect, the movement toward greater inter-Franciscan collaboration already has made significant strides. The Ministers General of the Friars Minor, Capuchins, Conventuals and Third Order Regular meet regularly to discuss matters of concern to the more than 40,000 friars they serve.

In the United States, the Franciscan Federation serves to inform and co-ordinate efforts of brothers and sisters of numerous Franciscan congregations of religious, men and women, counting nearly 30,000 members.

An Inter-Franciscan Congress on Mission, held in Mattli, Switzerland, in 1982, brought together Franciscans representing all the branches of the family on six continents to plan a joint effort in mission inspired by critical study of Franciscan sources.

The last twenty years also brought their share of difficulties. Membership in all branches of the Family declined. Tensions appeared between those demanding change and those critical of it. Yet through these difficulties a certain consensus emerged.

Common concerns and values animate members of the Franciscan Family throughout the world: the centrality of our life with God, the value of work and life with the poor, and the importance of community.

"The Spirit of Holy Prayer and Devotion"
(St. Clare)[1]

The foundation of Franciscan life is union with God. This demands of all Franciscans a serious commitment to the life of prayer and a constant return to the words of the Gospel as "spirit and life."

The Poor Clares have served the other members of the Family as constant reminders of the primacy of the search for God in Franciscan life. The enclosed, contemplative life of the Poor Clares continues to flourish in many places, and new Poor Clare communities in the Americas, Africa, Asia and Europe witness to the vitality of the Franciscan contemplative tradition today.

What is the life and work of the Poor Clares today? Their life has remained largely unchanged in its basic elements from the days of Clare herself. The communal celebration of the Liturgy of the Hours (the Divine Office) still marks the passing of the Poor Sisters' day from early in the morning until late at night with a special time dedicated to the celebration of the Eucharist. The sisters spend much of the day together—in the choir for liturgy, at meals, at community recreation, at work. The sisters rarely leave their monastery, and then usually for only a brief time for some necessary business. Their life remains the most intensely communal form of Franciscan living.

Their life also speaks to the rest of the Family of silence and personal solitude lived in community. The Poor Clare monastery is a quiet place. Talking and noise are limited. But the monastery is also a busy place. Each community is independent, financially and juridically. This demands work.

Some Poor Clare communities support themselves by

---

1   *Rule*, Chap. 7, in Armstrong-Brady, p. 219.

operating bakeries, producing bread for the Eucharist in many churches. Some support themselves with weaving and tailoring vestments and other liturgical furnishings. This work was one in which Clare herself was skilled, and many of her followers follow her example. Other communities, especially those in the countryside, engage in small-scale farming.

With their dedication to prayer, community, silence and work, the Poor Clares also show clearly the importance of joy in Franciscan life. Their life is a poor one, often relying on begging alms in order to pay bills when their work cannot fully support the community. Yet their life is neither somber nor sad. A visitor to a Poor Clare monastery will be received with a smiling courtesy that both Francis and Clare would expect of their followers.

From Malawi, an African Poor Sister speaks of the Franciscan message, its joy and its challenge:

> Franciscan life is not only a challenge to Franciscan women. It is, at the same time, a deep and wonderful meeting of many values which are rooted in traditional culture; for example, a strong feeling for community and sisterly life. May our Holy Founder St. Francis forgive us if we sometimes rival the crickets in our garden by celebrating joyfully and following his example. How thankful we are to God for giving us so great a Founder, who helps us, like a wonderful gardener, by means of his exceptional charm, to let the treasures of our culture unfold to the honor of God and the well-being of the Church![2]

While the Poor Clares are particularly dedicated to the

---

2   Mother M. Clare, OSC, "Herausforderungen an Franziskanische Schwestern in der Dritten Welt," Mattli, Switzerland (1982) 40, in *Charism* 5:17.

Franciscan contemplative life, other Franciscans are also pursuing this form of life. One result of the process of renewal since the Second Vatican Council has been a slow but steady return to the contemplative life among Franciscan friars.

Francis' *Rule for Hermitages* has inspired his brothers to live this form of life in different times and places. Those who study Franciscan history frequently observe that every period of renewal among the friars has given new life to the hermitages. The last twenty years provide evidence of this truth.

Whether in northern Italy, southern France or South Korea, friars are living today in hermitages. Their numbers are small, which is probably as it should be. Their importance is not measured in numbers. Usually in isolated places, the hermitages are marked by a silence, beauty and poverty that seem especially attractive today. According to the *Rule* written especially for them, these communities are always small—no more than a handful of friars. In the hermitages, the friars often begin (or end) the day at midnight, with the Office of Readings celebrated in common. From dawn until dark, the rest of the day is mostly lived in silence, with the celebration of the Hours in the choir, the Eucharist, two meals and manual labor filling the rest of the day. In many ways, the life of a friar in a hermitage today would probably seem familiar, at least in its essentials, to Francis and his early followers.

This renewed emphasis on the life of prayer is not limited to the Poor Clares and to friars. Other Franciscans, lay and religious, men and women, nourish the contemplative dimension of their lives. Some communities of Franciscan sisters have established "houses of prayer" or hermitages on their grounds, open to community members and others for a few days of contemplative renewal in the midst of a demanding and busy apostolate.

Members of the Secular Franciscan Order have also begun to explore the possibilities of the "hermitage life" for laypersons and their families.

Whether inside or outside a hermitage, wherever there are Franciscans, there is prayer. Each part of the Family has its own special ways of praying, but the celebration of the Liturgy, the Hours and the Eucharist remains a common denominator. Morning and evening, Franciscans gather to pray: two or three around a paraffin lamp on a road construction project in Bolivia; forty around an oil lamp in southern India; ten under a fluorescent tube in downtown Los Angeles. The contemplative dimension of Franciscan life remains fundamental to the life of the brothers and sisters of Francis and Clare.

"Work Faithfully and Devotedly" (St. Francis)[3]

Speaking from my own experience, I would like to mention here some of the more widely-known "works" of Franciscans. I do this with the awareness that only a summary, a "bird's-eye view," can be given in these pages. But it may be well to describe at least some of the more common forms of Franciscan work that the reader may know. Time and space will prevent me from mentioning here the musicians and artists, plumbers and marine biologists, the pediatricians and electricians, and all the thousands of unsung Franciscan workers who provide so much of the rich diversity of individual gifts that make up the Franciscan Family.

In his *Testament*, Francis recalled that he had always worked with his hands and wished to continue working. In the *Rule*, he spoke of work as a "grace," a gift from the Lord. He also asked

---

3   *Later Rule.* Chap. 5. Cf. Armstrong-Brady, p.140.

that each of his brothers know some skill or craft and have the tools necessary to carry it out.[4]

Franciscans today continue to work in many occupations. There are skilled Franciscan carpenters, engineers and architects. Some operate printing presses while others operate computers. Gardeners and wine-makers, cooks and tailors make up an important part of Franciscan communities. Their work is complemented by the ordinary tasks of administration performed by brothers and sisters at desks in offices. Yes, Franciscans also have to do their share of paperwork.

Franciscans are engaged in many forms of work. There is no single work that can be identified as *the* Franciscan work, or *the* Franciscan apostolate. Any honest occupation can be performed by a Franciscan. It is the way of working, and not the work itself, that expresses a Franciscan character. Marked by simplicity and generosity, centered on persons rather than products, "Franciscan" work can be seen in pulpits and potting-sheds, in a classroom and at a lathe.

Many readers may already know that Franciscans work as ministers in the Church. Franciscan priests serve in Catholic churches throughout the world. Through their ministry, in the Eucharist, the sacrament of reconciliation, preaching and counselling, they touch the lives of many. My own first contact with Franciscans came through my parish, Our Lady of Lourdes, in Seattle, Washington. Franciscans baptized me and heard my confession, taught me to be an altar boy, and eventually convinced me, as much by their example as by their words, that I might become a Franciscan myself.

My own story may be similar to that of others: my next point

---

4   *Testament*, no. 20, in Armstrong-Brady, p. 155; *Later Rule*, Chap. 5, *ibid.*, p. 140.

of contact with the Franciscans was at school. Franciscan sisters, of Glen Riddle (Philadelphia) taught me at the parish elementary school. Franciscans continue that ministry of education today. Such communities as the Franciscan Brothers of Brooklyn have a special dedication to the work of education. In a recent conversation with a friar of the Third Order Regular community, I learned that in the United States today there are more than twenty colleges and universities operated by Franciscans of both men's and women's communities. Franciscan women's communities in particular continue their work of education throughout the world today.

One form of work and ministry that remains a consistent concern of Franciscans is that of caring for society's poor. Many are familiar with hospitals with names like "St. Francis," "St. Elizabeth," and "St. Clare." Originally founded by Franciscan women's communities, these health-care facilities continue to serve the needs of the sick, especially those who are poor. From Francis' earliest days with victims of leprosy, care for the sick has retained an important place in the work of Franciscans.

Another phenomenon has marked these last few decades in the Franciscan ministry to the poor in the U.S. Members of the Secular Franciscan Order (Third Order) now operate a network of Franciscan centers throughout the country, places with different names, but a common purpose: to provide life's necessities to those who lack them. Food and clothing, hot coffee, a word of friendship: these are offered simply, often with referrals to other agencies for further help. The "Francis House" in downtown Seattle was my introduction to those Franciscans usually known as "Third Order members" twenty-five years ago. Working with them was my earliest day-to-day experience of the real life of the poor. The hard work of Franciscan laity there, men and women with families and jobs of their own, showed me the important services they provide for the poor, those locked out of the society of abundance.

In the popular imagination, this concern may be captured by the image of a kindly friar who distributes bread to the poor at the door of an ancient monastery. This work of charity remains universal in Franciscan houses. But another important aspect of Franciscan work is that of advocacy. Beyond direct assistance to the poor, Franciscans are involved today in working and living with the poor. This means participating in their struggle for human rights, for economic justice and its corollary, peace. Perhaps the most widely-known effort in this regard is the Latin American movement for ecclesial base communities (*comunidades de base*). Franciscans have played a role in this movement, and one of its primary spokesmen, Leonardo Boff, was a Franciscan friar, a leading author in the theology of liberation.

Franciscans are attempting to live in closer identification with the poor. The challenge of a "return to the sources" has made Franciscans reflect on positions of relative security and privilege they have acquired in many societies. The call to "opt for the poor," expressed in Church documents has become particularly important for Franciscans in recent years. This has meant for some the painful exchange of a relatively secure and profitable ministry in wealthy institutions for a more precarious life among the poor. It has entailed transferring the ownership and direction of prosperous institutions to the control of others in an attempt to live more and more "without property."

This option, not only to be "for" the poor, but with them, living as they live, has generated tensions in some places, but has also brought new vigor to the life of the Family. It has prompted significant efforts to denounce grave injustices borne by the poor in today's world. Moving beyond relief of the effects of injustice, Franciscan groups are today involved in the analysis of unjust social and economic systems. They participate in efforts to change structures that exploit the poor rather than concentrating only on necessary assistance.

A related and important Franciscan work is peace-making. The "Peace Prayer of St. Francis" summarizes for many the Franciscan call for peace. Although not found among the writings of the saint, this prayer certainly expresses some characteristics of Francis' life and action:

Lord, make me an instrument of Your peace.
Where there is hatred, let me sow love;
Where there is injury, pardon;
Where there is doubt, faith;
Where.there is despair, hope;
Where there is darkness, light;
And where there is sadness, joy.
O Divine Master, grant that I may not so much seek
To be consoled as to console;
To be understood as to understand;
To be loved as to love;
For it is in giving that we receive;
It is in pardoning that we are pardoned;
And it is in dying that we are born to eternal life.

Following the example of Francis, who strove to bring reconciliation to strife-torn Italian towns, Franciscan groups and individuals work for peace: Particular emphasis has been placed on the issues of nuclear weapons and the world-wide expense of armaments. Since these threaten life all over the globe, the halting of nuclear testing has become a widely-shared Franciscan concern in efforts toward peace.

Many associate Francis also with love for creatures and the natural world, remembering perhaps the annual blessing of animals at Franciscan churches on the Feast of St. Francis, October 4. Others have undoubtedly seen a statue of St. Francis presiding over a garden or a birdbath. Franciscan concern for nature today goes further than these symbols and gestures. The last decades have seen increasing Franciscan involvement in movements for preserving the integrity of creation. There is a growing awareness in today's world of threats to the environment from pollution, waste and unchecked industrial development. Remembering Francis' deep love for all creation, his calling earth "our Mother," and fire, wind and water, "brothers and sisters," Franciscans have begun to translate love and respect for creation into organized efforts for the protection of the natural world.

"And Show They are Members of the Same Family" (St. Francis)[5]

These varied forms of work and ministry call for the best energies of the brothers and sisters of the Franciscan Family. However, these activities would be only partially understood if seen as the private projects of individuals. To put work into its proper context, we should recall here the first component of Franciscan life, the life of prayer. That prayer takes place in a community. Work too must be understood in that communal

---

5   *Later Rule.* Chap. 6. Cf. Armstrong-Brady, p. 141.

context. Just as one's work supports the other brothers and sisters, their life of prayer and mutual encouragement supports the work of each. Whatever the work, it is shared through a community.

Franciscan communities of men and women, lay and religious, are organized in different ways, but with some common elements. These common features include a form of democratic government. Brothers and sisters are elected to positions of authority by the members of the community. They are frequently called "ministers" (servants) and "guardians." Their terms of office are fixed by law, and they can be removed by common consent. Decision-making is frequently centered in limited geographical areas (regions or provinces). In most branches of the Family, General Chapters or assemblies, composed of representatives from all the provinces, retain the highest authority and are responsible for electing the general administration of that part of the Family. With the title, "Minister General," or simply "President," one brother or sister is given overall authority and responsibility for a certain time, usually between four and six years.

In turn, each region or province has its own Provincial Chapter for the election of a "Provincial Minister" and the appointment of the heads of local communities, called "guardians" or "moderators." The local community may also have its own Chapter, a regular meeting of community members, to reflect on the Gospel together, and to make the necessary decisions for the community's life and the work of its members.

Franciscans pray, work, live among the poor and in a shared, common life. When speaking of the life and work of Franciscans today, the word "communion" may provide the best metaphor. The "founding charism" of the Family proposes communion with God as the bedrock of Franciscan life according to the Gospel.

God has first loved us, and we in turn are called to share that love, with God, with our "brothers and sisters," humans and all other creatures. God's own generous self-giving in becoming our fellow-creature in Jesus reveals the religious and spiritual meaning of our world. Work of various kinds is a way to participate in this creation. Work is a "grace," not a curse. To struggle for a just distribution of the gifts of God among all does not mean "mere politics" nor "mere social activism." Both political and social change affect the way in which our brothers and sisters live and are thus fundamentally religious and spiritual. So also are the work for peace, or for the integrity of creation—they are efforts toward greater communion of all creatures in the bountiful gifts of the Creator and an expression of love for the model of all creation, Christ.

This desire for communion underlies Franciscan life in community. By living as brothers and sisters in a shared life, Franciscans wish to experience a system of reciprocal relationships, based on mutuality and equality that are perceived as marking God's design for all creation. The purpose of that life is not to produce a more efficient team of workers, not to accomplish this or that task, however laudable. The goal of this life in communion is to include more and more brothers and sisters in its embrace, to reflect the origin and goal of all in the life of the Trinity.

Conclusion

In these pages I have assembled a series of snapshots, pieces of a family portrait, that of the Franciscans. I hope that the reader may now have some notion of the family's members, their stories and their spirit. Much remains to be said, and it is my hope that others will be moved by this imperfect sketch to fill in some of the empty spaces, to tell the untold stories. At least the reader may now have a better idea of the richness of Francis' and Clare's gift to the Church. Through the last eight centuries their followers have multiplied and divided, moving out from their original Umbrian home to nearly every country in the world today.

It is my hope that the reader has been informed, inspired, or even amused by some of the stories told here and will forgive much that was imperfect in the telling. These pages are a gift to my Franciscan brothers and sisters and to the many others who have felt the attraction of the Franciscan vision.

As the brothers and sisters of Francis and Clare carry into the twenty-first century the heritage they have received, they do it in response to Francis' own prayer for us all: "May the Lord give you peace."[6]

---

6   *Testament.* no. 23, in Armstrong-Brady, p.155.

Subject Index

A

Ad Statum, 64

Africa, North, 95, 151

Agnes (of Assisi), St., 8, 14

Agnes (of Prague), Bl., 21ff.

Albert of Pisa, 25

Alcantarines, 70

Alessandro of Alessandria, 56

Alexander of Hales, 130, 142

Alfonso de Madrid, 145

alter Christus, 62

Ambrose, 20

Americas, 70, 82, 101, 103, 152, 160

Angelina da Marsciano, 99

Angelo Clareno, 43, 44, 52, 53, 56, 57, 58

Angelo of Rieti, 43

Anglican Church, 115

Anglican Franciscans, 116

Anthony of Padua, St., viii, 38, 142

Antonine of Florence, St., 101

"apostolic life," 48, 49

Arbor vitae crucifixae Iesu, 55

Armenia, 52, 57

Asia, Southeast, 95

Assisi, 1, 2, 3, 5, 6, 7, 8, 9, 10, 11, 12, 14, 17, 18, 20, 24, 36, 58, 67, 84, 88, 99, 109, 110, 157

Auspicato concessum, 111

Australia, 95

B

Bachmann, Frances, 113

Bartholomew of Pisa, 62

Basilica of St. Francis (Assisi), 109

Battista Varani, 83

Beatrice de Silva, 82

Beghards, 99

Beguines, 56, 98, 99

Belgium, 10, 82, 92, 93, 98, 99

Benedict XIII, Pope, 81

Benedictines, 9ff, 15, 23, 49

Benoit de Canfield (William Fitch), 145

Bentivoglio, Maria Maddalena, 93

Berger, Anna Katherine, 115

Bernard de Bustis, 101

Bernard of Quintavalle, 6, 43

Bernardine of Feltre, 80

Bernardine of Laredo, 145

Bernardine of Siena, 63, 64, 80, 101

Bernardino of Portogruaro, 93

bizzocchi, 56

bizzoche, 8

Boff, Leonardo, 166

Boll, Margaret, 113, 114

Bologna, 12, 24, 38, 93, 141

Bonagratia of Bergamo, 57

Bonaventura da Caltagirone, 72, 74

Bonaventure of Bagnoreggio, St., 19, 22, 27, 42, 44, 79, 120, 130, 131, 132, 136, 139, 142

Boniface VIII, Pope, 53

Bons-Fils, 102

Borneo, 95

Boulier, Martial, 70

Brazil, viii, 106, 152

Brothers and Sisters of Penance, iv, 7, 10, 16, 18, 19, 20, 32, 97, 98, 100, 104, 106, 108, 116, 139, 158, (see also Penitents)

Burma, 95

Burton, M. Frances, 113

C

Canada, 93, 95, 152

Canons Regular, 49

Canterbury, 141

"Canticle of Brother Sun," 12, 13

Capestrano Rule, 19, 20

Capuchin Poor Clares, 89, 92

Capuchins (Friars Minor), 32, 56, 67ff, 70, 84, 94, 95, 103

Capuchos, 68

Caro of Florence, 20

Caterina Cybo (Duchess of Camerino), 75

Caterina de' Vigri, St., of Bologna, 83

Celestine V, Pope, 53

Chappotin de Neuville, Elena, 115

Chapter, General, 99, 100, 103, 169; (Padua), 42; (Paris), 42, 73; (Pisa), 42; (Toledo), 106; (Venice), 59

Chapter of Definitors, 26

Chapter of Utrecht, 100

Chapter, Provincial, 71, 169

Chateaubriand, 109

China, 90, 151

Christmas, 41, 122, 134, 140, 141

Christocentrism, 129, 132

Christology, 131, 132

Cismontanes, 66, 67

Cistercians, 9, 20

"Civil Constitution of the Clergy," 108

Clare, St. *passim*

Clement V, Pope, 55

Clement VI, Pope, 59

Clement VII, Pope, 71

Clement VIII, Pope 72, 74, 75

Clement XI, Pope, 102

Colettan friars, 82

Colette of Corbie, (Nicolette Boellet), St., 81, 82, 83, 91, 92, 93

Colettines, 82, 85, 92, 95

Columbus, 152

Community, 45, 59

Company of St. Ursula, 102

comunidades de base, 166

Conceptionists, 82

"Conformities," 62, 63

Congregations of the Most Blessed
Sacrament, 107

Conrad of Offida, 44

contemplation, 36, 39, 93, 96, 139

contemplative communities, 68, 99

Conventuals, (Friars Minor) 32, 65, 66,
82, 109, 116

Cordier, Veronica, 113

Council, (Lateran IV), 8, 17, 49, 98;
(Lyons), 47; (
Trent), 104, 105;
(Vienne), 99;
(Vatican II), 95, 155, 162

Council, Third Plenary (Baltimore),
112

creation, 131, 132, 168, 170

creatures, 121, 122, 126

Crescentius of Iesi, 21, 26

Crete, 85

Cross, 136

Crucified, 135

Crusade, 1, 10, 11, 84, 150

Cum inter nonnullos, 57

Cyprus, 85

D

Damietta, 10, 11, 24

De Marche, Maria, 93

Der heilige Franziskus von Assisi:
Ein Troubadour, 109

Discalced friars. 69, 70, 75

Domenica, M. Maria, 92

Dominicans, 25, 65, 101

Dorn, Bernardine, 113, 114

Doyle, Eric, 129, 130

E

Egypt, 41, 94

Elias Bombarone, 12, 19, 25

Elizabeth of Hungary, St., 99, 110

Elizabethines, 99, 102, 106

Erasmus, 86, 143

eremitical life, 32, 61, 67, 71, 78, 89

Esser, Kajetan, 157

Eucharist, 123, 136, 137, 160ff

"Exhortation to the Brothers and
Sisters of Penance," 7

Expositio quattuor magistrorum, 26

Extremadura, 67, 69

F

Falconio, Diomede, 116

Farinier, William, 59

Farnese, Maria Francesca, 89

Favarone di Offreduccio, 7

Fioretti, 110

Florida, 152

Foligno, 58, 59, 60, 99

Fonte Colombo, 12, 140

forma vitae, 6, 9

de Foucauld, Charles, 94

France, 22, 23, 24, 73, 74, 81, 82, 87, 89,
91, 93, 94, 95, 98, 99, 100, 102,
105, 106, 107, 108, 142

Francia, 10

Francis, St., *passim*

Franciscan Brothers of Brooklyn, 165

Franciscan Federation, 157, 159

Franciscan Poets in Italy, 110
Franciscan Sisters (Allegany), 113;
(Belle Prairie), 115;
(Braintree), 113;
(Clinton), 114;
(Dubuque), 114;
(East Peoria), 114;
(Joliet), 115;
(Little Falls), 115;
(Maryville), 115;
(Milwaukee), 113;
(Oldenburg), 113;
(of Penance and Charity), 113;
(Philadelphia), 114, 115, 165;
(Rochester), ll4;
(Rock Island), 115;
(St. Louis), 114, 115;
(Sylvania), 114;
(Syracuse), 114;
(Tiffin), 114;
(Williamsville), 114
Franciscanophiles, 110
Francisco de Osuna, 145
fraticelli, 53, 56, 57, 62, 99
fratres simplices, 62
Friars Minor (see Lesser Brothers)

G

Gemelli, Agostino, 31
Gentile of Spoleto, 58, 59, 61
Geraldus Odonis, 59
Germany, 41, 71, 73, 74, 98, 99, 102, 105ff, 111, 114
Giesen, Maria Augustine, 115
Giles, 6, 10, 43, 44
Giovanni da Fano, 75

Goerres, Josef, 109
Gonzaga, Francesco, 72, 73, 85
Grand Couvent, 142, 144
Grandmontines, 49
Gray Penitents, 102
Gray Sisters, 99
Great Schism, 100
Greccio, 41, 44, 122, 140
Greece, 53, 57
Gregory IX, Pope, (see Ugolino)
Gregory X, Pope, 47
Gregory XI, Pope, 62
Gregory of Naples, 24
Guadalupenses, 68
Guido, 3

H

Hackelmeier, Theresa, 113
Hayes, Elizabeth, 115
Hayes, Zachary, 131
Haymo of Faversham, 25ff
Helyot, Hippolyte, 107
Henry de Herp (Harphius), 143
hermitage, 138ff, 162, 163
hermits, 4, 37, 94, 101, 103, 138
Hermits of Pope Celestine, 53
History of the Seven Tribulations…, 57
Holland, 98, 106, 114
Holy Land, 84 (Custody of), 151
Honorius III, Pope, 9, 12, 19
Hospital Sisters, 99

I

Illuminato, 10, 24
Incarnation, 122, 127, 128, 132, 133, 134
India, 95
Innocent III, 6, 8, 49

Innocent IV, Pope, 15, 21ff

International Franciscan Conference, 157

Ireland, 97, 107, 108

Iriarte, Lázaro, 30, 67

Isabel of France, 23, 83

Islam, 150

Ite vos, 65

J

Jacques de Vitry, 17, 18, 36

James of Massa, 44

Jansenism, 91

Japan, 95, 96, 151

Java, 95

Jean de la Rochelle, 142

Jesuits, 95, 146

John Capistran, St., 80, 82, 101

John of Cappella, 24

John of Parma,19, 22, 26, 44

John of Valle, 58, 59, 61

John Parenti, 19, 25

John XXII, Pope, 56, 57, 98

Juan de la Puebla, 67, 70

Juan de Guadalupe, 68

Juan Pascual, 69

Julius II, Pope, 101

K

Kulturkampf, 111, 114

L

La Verna, 12, 36, 37, 41, 55, 140

Lawrence of Brindisi, St., 145

Lent(s), 7, 140, 141

Leo X, Pope, 64, 69, 75, 82, 102, 103, 104, 107

Leo XIII, Pope, 20, 111

Leonard de Paris, 107

Leo, 43

Leonardo of Giffoni, 62

lepers, xi, 4, 5, 7, 24, 36, 98, 125, 134

Lesser Brothers (Friars Minor), 7ff, 24ff, 29ff

"Letter to All the Faithful," 10

"Letter to Brother Leo, "34

Libya, 85

Lichetto, Francesco, 70, 85

Life of Clare, 8

Life of Francis, 42; (Second), 42

Limburg Reform, 106

Liturgy of the Hours, 160

loci, 36

Lockhart, M. Elizabeth, 113

Longo, Maria Lorenza, Ven., 89

Ludovico da Fossombrone, 75ff

Ludwig of Einsiedeln, 105

Luther, Martin, 65, 86

M

Malawi, vii, xi, 161

Manila, ix, x, 90

Manzoni, 110

Marches of Ancona, 6, 44, 48, 51, 53, 75

Maria de Agreda, Ven., 88

Maria Theresa, Empress of Austria, 108

Martinengo, Maria Maddalena, 88

Mary, (Blessed Virgin), 136, 137

Matteo da Basci, 75, 77

Matthew of Narni, 24

Memoriale propositi, 18

Merici, Angela, St., 102

Mexico, 107, 111, 152

Michael of Cesena, 56, 57

Michelet, 109

Minims, 102

Mission, 146ff

Moes, Alfreda, 113, 114

moniales, 8

Montalembert, 110

Monte Mesma, 31, 32

Monticelli, 14

Morocco, 24, 95

Movimento Religiose Francescane, 157

Muslim, 150, 151

Mussar, Vincent, 107

N

nature, 168

Near East, 10, 24, 41, 84, 151

Neerinckx, Jeanne, 106

Neumann, John, St., 113

Nicholas IV, Pope, 20, 98, 102, 104

Nicholas V, Pope, 100

Nimmo, Duncan, 33, 34, 41, 43, 45

Nuremberg, 86

O

Obregon, Bernardino, 102

Obregones, 102

Observants (Friars Minor), 32, 33, 58ff, 63ff, 72ff, 78, 80, 104, 144

O'Fallon, Ellen, 113

Olivi, Peter John, 55

O'Neill, Ann, 113

Ortolana, 7

Oxford, 38, 141

Ozanam, Frederick, 110

P

Paolo da Chiozza, 77

Paolo da Soncino, 70

Paolo (Paoluccio) dei Trinci, 58ff

Paris, 38, 42, 73, 92, 102, 141, 142, 144

Paul III, Pope, 103

Paul VI, Pope, 158

peace, 116, 156, 166, 167, 168, 170, 171

"Peace Prayer of St. Francis," 167

Penitents, iv, ix, 4, 7, 8, 10, 17ff, 27, 66, 98, 99, 101, 102, 106, 151

Perugia, 2

Peter Cattaneo, 6, 12, 24, 25

Peter of Alcantara, St., 69, 89, 145

Pfanneregg Reform, 105

Philippines, 70, 90, 152

Pietro da Fossombrone, 52

Pietro da Macerata, 52

Pirkheimer, Charitas, 86

Pius V, Pope, 103, 104

Pius VII, Pope, 92, 109

Pius XI, Pope, 94

Poor Sisters, (Poor Clares) 8, 10, 14ff, 27, 66, 79ff, 100, 139, 157, 160ff

Portugal, 24, 68, 69, 70, 101, 102, 103, 107, 108, 142

Porziuncola, 5, 6, 14, 24, 36, 41

poverty, 38, 42, 43, 45, 46, 82, 87, 88, 106, 109

Prague, 21

Prayer, 5, 6, 8, 10, 36, 37, 54, 58, 61, 84, 92, 98, 137, 139, 140, 141, 149, 160, 162, 163, 167, 168, 169, 171

"privilege of poverty," 9, 14

Proto-Monastery (of St. Clare, Assisi), 79, 84

Q

Quiñones, Francisco, 70

*Quo elongati,*25, 45, 46, 47
R
Rabelais, 143
Radermacher, Apollonia, 106
Raffaele da Fossombrone, 76ff
Raymond, Goedfroy, 55
Raynald of Segni, 14, 15, 22
Recollects, 73, 74
Recollectine Penitents, 106
Recollectines, 106
Reformation, Protestant, 33, 86, 90, 101, 108
Reformed friars, 32, 64ff
religionis zelus, 78
Renan, Ernest, 110
retiros, 67, 68, 71
Revolution, French, 90, 91, 92, 111
Revolution, Industrial, 112
riformati (see Reformed friars)
Rimini, 19
Romantic Movement, 109, 156
Rome, 3, 6, 25, 26, 64, 70, 75, 76, 86, 89
Rufino, 7, 8, 43
Rule, (of Lesser Brothers) 9, 12, 25ff, 49; (of Leo X), 102, 103, 104, 107; (of Nicholas IV), 98, 102, 103; (of St. Augustine), 49; (of St. Benedict), 9, 15, 49; (of Paul III), 103; (of Penitents), 18; (of Poor Sisters), 9, 12, 14ff, 96; (of the Third Order), 98, 99, 101, 102, 104; (of Urban IV), 70, 89
S
Sabatier, Paul, 110

Saint-Omer Reform, 105
"Salutation of the Virgin," 136
San Damiano, 3, 5, 8, 9, 14, 15, 20, 21, 22, 79
Sancta romana, 56
Sanctitas vestra, 54
Sant 'Angelo in Panzo, 8
Scotus, John Duns, 88, 120, 130, 132, 133, 134, 145
Secular Franciscan Order, x, 158, 163, 165 (see also Brothers and Sisters of Penance, Third Order)
Serra, Junipero, Bl., 152
Siena, 12
Sisters of Mercy, 102
Sixtus IV, Pope, 101
Sixtus V, Pope, 103
Social Impact of Franciscanism, 109
Society of the Atonement, 115
Society of St. Francis, 116
Society of St. Vincent de Paul, 110
sorores minores inclusae, 23
Spain, 22, 24, 25, 67, 68, 69, 70, 72, 75, 82, 88, 89, 100, 101, 102, 103, 107, 108, 111, 143
Spalding, John Lancaster, 115
Spiltzlin, Elizabeth, 105
Spirituals, 26, 27, 33, 42ff, 52, 54ff, 59, 68
Spoleto, 3, 58
Stendhal, 109
stigmata, 12, 41
Strict Observance, 107
Stricter Observance, 58, 61, 80, 105
Subasio, Mt., 6

Sultan, 10, 11, 23, 24, 151

Supra montem, 2

Switzerland, 31, 105, 159

Sylvester, 8, 10, 139

Syria, 10, 57, 84

T

Taffin, Françoise, 105

Taiwan, 151

Teresa of Avila, St., 145

Tertiaries, 98, 100, 101, 102, 106, 107, 108, 113

Testament (of St. Francis), 4, 5, 6, 41, 42, 43, 45, 46, 47, 55, 163

Thailand, 95

Third Order, iv, 97, 98, 101, 102, 104, 106, 107, 108, 110, 111, 116, 147, 157, 158, 165

Third Order Regular, iv, 83, 89, 97, 101, 108, 147, 157, 158, 159, 165

Third Order Secular (see Secular Franciscan Order)

Thomas of Celano, 3, 8, 25, 26, 42, 49

Todd, Mary Joan, 113

Tommaso da Castel d'Emilio, 52

Tommaso da Tolentino, 52

Tommaso of Foligno, 58

Tremblay, Joseph du, 107

Trinity, 120, 121, 123, 133, 170

U

Ubertino da Casale, 44, 54

Ugolino, Cardinal, (Pope Gregory IX), 9, 10, 14, 15, 18, 20, 21, 25, 45, 50, 151

Ultramontanes, 66, 67

United States, 93, 113, 116, 152, 153, 157, 159, 165

Urban IV, Pope, 23, 80, 89

Urbanists, Royal, 89

usus pauper, 54

V

Vaast, Adelaide, 113

Veronica Giuliani, St., 88

Vie de S. François, 110

Viganega, Benedetta Wanherten, 105

vita evangelica, 137

von Hase, Karl, 110

W

Wadding, Luke, 145

Wattson, Paul, 115

Way of the Cross, 134

White, Lurana Mary, 115

William of Ockham, 57

work, 163

X

Ximenes, Francisco, Cardinal, 83, 142

Y

Yves de Paris,107

Z

Zahler, Ottilia Duerr, 113

Zepperen, Congregation of, 100

Zumarraga, Juan de, 107